The Science of Discipline

The Science of Discipline

8 Strategies for Empowering Educators and Engaging Students

Nathan Maynard

JB JOSSEY-BASS™
A Wiley Brand

Published by John Wiley & Sons, Inc., Hoboken, New Jersey.

ISBNs: 9781394253500 (Cloth), 9781394254071 (ePDF), 9781394254064 (ePub).

Library of Congress Cataloging-in-Publication Data:

Cover Design: Paul McCarthy
Cover Images: © Getty Images | Klaus Vedfelt
Printed and bound by CPI Group (UK) Ltd, Croydon, CR0 4YY
C9781394253500_300126

To my grandfather, Bruce Costa,
and the lessons he taught me.

To my son, Asher Maynard, and the future he
reminds me to believe in.

Contents

Introduction

Kids will sacrifice love to feel part of a group. Belonging gives them security and identity that they crave.

"Maynard, I need you in room 333!" was the only thing I heard on my walkie-talkie, as a teacher called for administrator assistance.

I walked in to find the teacher at the front of the class, arms crossed, the room at a quiet standstill. Clearly frustrated, she pointed at a student toward the back and loudly said, "If you were at a different school, you would be dragged out of here in handcuffs for acting like this! Get him out of here."

My head snapped toward the teacher, embarrassed that every student had just heard this. I quickly turned my back to the class and, to avoid making her feel called out, softly said, "Do not say that. That will make this harder. What is going on?"

She pointed again at the student, "Gage is refusing to do anything. He needs to leave." Hearing this, the student chuckled and swirled around in his chair, pulling his hood over his head as he texted.

Even as I walked over to his desk, he continued tapping away and would not look at me. I asked him to come out and talk in the hallway. No response.

I edged closer and said, "I really don't know what's going on, but I want to figure it out with you. Come out in the hallway with me."

"Nope," he said nonchalantly.

I could feel the situation was close to escalating. The teacher continued to make provoking comments, and the class was starting to engage. Some students laughed softly, some shook their heads, while others looked the other way in frustration—but the one thing no one was doing was learning.

Turning to Gage, I quietly said, "I'll give you two options, and I really hope you choose the first one. One, you can come out in the hallway and chat with me. I'll give you two minutes to finish what you're doing and meet me there."

Then I offered him the second option with an assertive but calm tone, "Option two isn't going to be fun for either of us, but I'll have to hang out over there until you're ready to leave the class to chat with me," I said, pointing to a corner in the classroom. "But if you go with option two, I will want you to make up the time that you took away from my day."

After more ignoring and swirling in his chair, he held up a "1" with his finger as he continued to text. I said, "Appreciate it. It's 10:30 right now. I'll see you at 10:32 right over there," pointing outside the classroom. I walked past the teacher and said, "I got this, if you want to get your lesson going again." The teacher gave me a drained look. I then walked out into the hallway, where I could still see what was going on but was far enough away not to further antagonize the teacher, the classroom, and him.

Slightly after the two-minute mark, he walked out to join me.

I asked why he had his phone out in class and what was going on. He didn't make eye contact with me or speak much, but he had put his phone in his pocket.

He then said, "Can we go to your office?" I brought him down the hall into my office.

I asked again, "So tell me what's going on?"

He continued to look at the floor and sat quietly for a few minutes before saying, "I'm texting my sister; we have stuff to figure out."

"What type of stuff? Cell phones aren't something you can use in class, even if it's something important."

Gage kept looking down and then softly said, "My mom died."

My heart sank.

He began to open up as we chatted and told me that his mother had tragically died and now he had to make arrangements to live with his slightly older sister. It took every ounce of energy I had not to cry. This young man was navigating one of the most traumatizing events he's ever experienced, and a teacher had just threatened, in front of the entire class with me in the classroom too, to drag him out of a classroom in handcuffs.

Did this excuse him for being noncompliant with the teacher and ignoring her? *No.*

Did this readjust how I handled this discipline situation? *Absolutely.*

Gage didn't tell anyone at school what happened to his mother. If he had, as his guidance counselor, I could have created a support plan for when he felt overwhelmed in class. Instead, he chose not to draw attention to himself—he was pursuing the feeling of belonging.

Let's say that if I hadn't come down in time, or hadn't ask questions, that this situation might have gone differently. What if Gage's behavior escalated after hearing the comment about being "dragged out of his classroom in handcuffs" while trying to handle living arrangements and processing the loss of the closest person in his life? What if he flipped over a desk and cussed at the teacher as he walked out of the class? What if he had shouldered another student or even me as he walked out?

Similar situations like this provoke students and escalate the issue, leading to a significant number of students suspended and arrested in schools. This is one of the drivers of the school-to-prison pipeline.

A fact was that Gage was a Black male, and the teacher was white. Implicit bias has been studied and is real. This was a situation that could have changed Gage's life but wouldn't have changed the teacher's life even though she had threatened arrest over a slight disruption.

Many teachers struggle to recognize how implicit bias shapes their own perceptions of students (Breese et al., 2023). I've often also heard teachers say, "I don't know if I have it or not, but I don't want to," and most feel unsure what to do about it. What I've found is that it's most important to recognize that our state of mind strongly influences how much implicit bias "leaks out." When people are stressed, angry, anxious, tired, or emotionally dysregulated, the brain tends to rely more on automatic or unconscious shortcuts. So we must strive to be regulated, even when triggered by a student's behavior. After this teacher reprimanded Gage inappropriately, the first thing I recognized after looking around the room was that several other students were also on their phones.

My goal is for this book to help you navigate the hard, the complex, the unengaged, and the frustrating behaviors that create harm. We will also unpack the science behind behavior together so you understand what is happening in these difficult moments and ways to take action.

We will do this, though, through the lens of empathy. We believe that kids deserve to be heard, seen, and understood as their authentic selves, even when they act out. Throughout this book, you will learn how to create connected relational learning communities, from the classroom to your full school culture. You will learn from experts around the world, recent data, and my lived experiences.

Discipline doesn't have to be painful. Discipline has to teach and focus on seeking to understand what is behind the behavior. What is the driver of the behavior? You don't go to the mechanic with a smoking engine and expect them to only inflate your tires—they seek to find and address the real issue. This is why every chapter will begin with a story that illustrates many of the different challenges you and your students may face in the classroom and the science behind the practices.

My hope is that this book becomes your guide for discipline that holds accountable negative behavior, builds empathy, and helps you strengthen relationships during the process. This book is built around real stories, anonymized to respect everyone involved, to show you honest situations you may have been in yourself or may want to know how to handle in the future.

What's Not Working

Removing students for small negative behaviors from their educational environment does more harm than good. It rocks a student's ability to feel safe in the space, knowing that, at any point, they can be removed again. This is an example of an intentional or unintentional "fear-based" driver. It is also hard for the student to reintegrate into the classroom community after being removed. Data shows that being removed for minor misbehaviors negatively affects students' educational trajectories and often shapes lifelong beliefs about themselves. Research indicates that students who are suspended or expelled are nearly three times more likely to come into contact with the juvenile justice system the following year. These points help us understand why we need progressive accountability consequences in the classroom that teach and seek to understand the driver of the behavior.

When was the last time you were kicked out of a staff meeting for talking too much to another educator or being on your cell phone? I'm guessing never. If you did get kicked out of the staff meeting though, do you think it would be easy to show up next time and act like nothing happened around your colleagues?

Every interaction we have with a student communicates something, whether spoken or unspoken. Removing a student from the classroom can send the message that they don't belong, that they are not capable of mending their mistakes, and that this environment isn't safe for them to bring their full selves. This is the message many punitive practices are sending to our kids. Instead, we need to empathize deeply when we interact with children so we understand what they might be going through and can help them process the situation fully.

This book isn't a magic solution to all disciplinary challenges. Instead, it's a comprehensive guide to maintaining peace in your classroom, fostering a climate of respect, and building a culture of positive behavior through proven, effective methods. We'll explore and build on restorative justice practices that help students learn from their mistakes, repair harm, and continue forward in a supportive environment.

Restorative practices focus on building the skill of empathy for kids and adults. There is a common belief that empathy is a soft approach to teaching, even a distraction, but empathy is the strongest skill we can develop to reduce violence and harmful behavior. It helps you and your students understand how someone else is feeling, which can reduce conflict and build better relationships. It allows us to identify with the harm caused and find ways to resolve it. So why isn't this skill a focal point for all discipline?

Every day is a new chance to connect with *all* students and especially your most challenging kids. These students are used to people giving up on them. By holding them accountable while showing relentless kindness and encouragement, we can make a real impact. Instead of the outdated "carrot and stick" approach, reward systems, or fear of punishment, this book will teach you how to create intrinsic motivation and a classroom where kids take ownership of their behavior and learning.

Supported by modern research in behavioral neuroscience; my years as a youth worker, teacher, and school administrator; and my experience working directly with thousands of students and educators across the world, I will walk you through eight restorative strategies that have transformed some of the most complicated school systems and classrooms:

1. **Understanding behavior:** Seek to understand the driver behind behaviors.

2. **Building belonging:** Create an inclusive environment where every student feels valued and connected.

3. **Increasing accountability:** Teach kids to take responsibility for their actions through clear expectations and consistent consequences.

4. **Leading with empathy:** Encourage understanding and sharing of feelings to foster a compassionate community.

5. **Teaching self-regulation:** Introduce kids to three keys to manage stress and practice coping skills.

6. **Modeling respect:** De-escalate and manage difficult behaviors with respect and learn effective strategies to maintain a safe environment.

7. **A framework for forgiveness:** Stop labeling the "bad kid," give your students tools to repair the harm, and start fresh.

8. **Empowering differentiated thinking:** Support all students—especially the neurodivergent and disabled students with personalized and inclusive teaching practices.

We know our job is cut out for us with the rise of the "anxious generation" and students feeling lonelier than ever. The ability to access information rapidly and push through algorithms can radicalize and polarize thinking. Recent data reveal a concerning rise in anxiety and loneliness among youth. In the United States, 16.1% of adolescents ages 12–17 have a diagnosed anxiety disorder—an increase of 61% from 2016 to 2023—while approximately 20% report symptoms of anxiety or depression (CDC, 2023). On a global scale, around 25% of teens aged 15–18 say they often or very often feel lonely (World Health Organization, 2023), and among Gen Z more broadly, up to 73% report feeling lonely at least sometimes. These trends highlight a growing mental health crisis among young people, as research consistently links early loneliness and anxiety with long-term emotional and psychological challenges.

In a world where kids face information overload, social media pressures, constant exposure to global tragedies, and the lure of rapidly evolving technology, we need discipline strategies that are as dynamic and resilient as our students. This book provides the tools to build a supportive, positive school culture where every student can thrive.

Let's reimagine school discipline. Let's create environments where students feel heard, understood, and empowered to make better choices. With responsible and caring discipline, we can help launch our students into a healthier headspace, leading to more productive and fulfilling lives. Every student deserves adults who care about them. Restorative practices are the key to creating a sense of peace and belonging in every school.

Who Am I?

Like with Gage, we never know what a student is facing at home or in their community, in addition to the societal pressures they carry. The trauma-informed strategies in this book will help you understand the lives of kids who are fighting silent battles and help you be better equipped to deal with kids who are struggling the most, kids like me.

I was raised by a family where discipline was harsh. Before the age of 13, I had also experienced trauma with 9 out of 10 adverse childhood experiences (ACEs). I didn't really fit in at school, or with my family, and felt disconnected from my community and continued to act out. I was often labeled as troubled or at-risk. In seventh grade, searching for a place to belong, I started to be pulled into criminal behaviors, and this only led to more poor decisions.

School was not important to me. I believe I was sent to the office 73 times, something the principal would tally on a sticky note he had stuck to his desk; reading this from a journal I had from middle school opened my eyes to how much disruption I was causing around me. I had become desensitized to consequences and was headed down a tough road. I was being raised to be tough, but I was young and trying to understand the world with little nurturing.

Then one teacher forever changed my path in eighth grade by explaining how a good GPA could help me get into college and allow me to do what I wanted with my life. He showed me that I had options and agency to direct my own future. Even with behavioral challenges along the way, this fueled me to graduate high school, go to Purdue University, and get a degree in behavioral neuroscience.

I started my career at the favorite place I've ever worked: a juvenile residential treatment care center, where I came face-to-face with some of the most misunderstood youth in my community—kids labeled violent, broken, or lost. Kids with criminal records, homeless, or needing a safe space. Seeing myself in these kids opened my eyes and gave me a deeper understanding of my own story.

For nearly a decade, I worked inside the juvenile justice system in Tippecanoe County, Indiana; my first three years, I worked directly on the violent offender and sexually maladaptive unit. I then became the clinical case manager, supporting reintegration into the community, and worked directly with the local schools. I learned how to build relationships, mentor, and hold accountable some of the highest need students in the state. When the youth themselves voted me as Indiana's "Youth Worker of the Year," after seven years of working at the treatment care center, it wasn't just an honor; it was validation that healing is possible through this work.

I realized throughout this time that the real transformation for youth had to happen before the justice system ever got involved—in the schools.

I transitioned into education, first with adult students at The Excel Center, where I started teaching and led college and career readiness. I was then promoted into an assistant principal "Lead Life Coach" position. There, I created the "Keys to Success" discipline model—a restorative, progressive, simple classroom accountability system. It gave teachers simple steps to follow to embrace forgiveness and repair harm after a misbehavior. It wasn't a theory. It was working. Suspensions dropped. Teachers felt more equipped. And then the system scaled across all the other 13 Excel Center schools in Indiana.

Then I was given the opportunity to help build something from the ground up. The vision was to have a high school that "reimagined education" but focused on supporting underserved and underprivileged students across Indianapolis. We set out to design a project-based, STEM-focused approach that would engage students in innovative, hands-on ways. I joined the team building Purdue Polytechnic High School (PPHS) and became one of the founding administrators at the first building. My main role as the Dean, was school discipline. Our school had the lowest suspension and recidivism rates in all of Marion County schools. Later after I left, PPHS class of 2022 students overwhelmingly outperformed students across Indianapolis high schools on the state tests given to eleventh graders in 2021. PPHS students were also four times as likely to pass both the math and English sections of the test as students in IPS (34 versus 8%). A discipline model that was built around teaching empathy was working and showing increased academic successes with the multifaceted approach the school was built upon.

Founder of TeacherGoals and educator Brad Weinstein was hired in the middle of our first year of PPHS, where he joined our district office. He quickly saw the way we handled discipline with success. I remember clearly the day he met with me after school and said, "I think you need to write a book about this." He then told me how he used to use circles as a teacher and some of the restorative discipline work he did as a school administrator. So, we developed a plan to write *Hacking School Discipline* together.

I hoped the book would help some educators and maybe help me pay down some of my debt—I had no idea how successful it would go on to become.

Despite receiving criticism that the book might not resonate, it quickly became a bestseller, reaching #6 in the world for all nonfiction books, selling more than 250,000 copies around the world. As my reputation grew, I was invited to work in some of the most complex school environments in the United States in Brooklyn, Youngstown, Chicago, Bakersfield, Los Angeles, Arlington, Washington, DC, Indianapolis, Memphis, and many cities listed with the highest rates of violence and other complexities.

The same year the book launched in 2017, I also founded a company called BehaviorFlip, where I co-launched the first restorative behavior management app. After partnering with more than 300 schools and reaching 90,000 monthly users, we found we were achieving outcomes we could measure, from reduced suspensions to increased attendance. Then in 2022, I launched Highfive, with the mission to create connected school communities that teach empathy and forgiveness with discipline. Merging BehaviorFlip with my consulting work, we built a trauma-informed tool to become a "behavior coach in your pocket," a classroom app, and a new model for scaling progressive consequences and measuring belonging. Within a year, Highfive quickly earned national recognition—winning EdTech Week's award for The Most Innovative K–12 Company.

Through all of it, my purpose has remained steady. I believe every human strives to feel like they belong and deserves to feel belonging while being seen and heard. I also believe, from my journey and experiences, that the best way to proactively address negative behavior and violence is by teaching empathy.

1

Understanding What's Behind the Behavior

Why Kids Act Out and Punitive Punishment Doesn't Work

"Traditional discipline works with the kids that need it the least, but it works the least with the kids that need it the most."
—**Dr. Lori Desautels**

Seek to Understand: The Reason Underneath the Pattern

Every school I go to, I always hear about their most challenging student. I get the multiyear stories and hear about the significant efforts that are made to help this specific student. I see the pain

1

on the faces of the educators looking for answers. They want to receive the "magic wand" strategy that will change everything and reveal what they might have missed. This is what the educators were looking for with Waya.

Waya was in fourth grade, and every morning at drop off, he was escorted by two adults from his parents' car to his "classroom." His classroom was a padded de-escalation room. The educators explained that this room was necessary and part of his individualized plan due to Waya's intense outbursts, multiple elopement attempts per day, and inability to be around others.

The school served students from two competing Native American tribes cohabiting on the same reservation. While supporting the school, I would stay at a casino on the reservation, and one time asked the hotel's employees a few questions. The crime and violence they described on the reservation far surpassed anything I heard about—even compared to some of the top rated "violent" cities that I've worked in. "Why do the two tribes stay on the same reservation even when they don't get along?" I asked.

The lady smiled and chuckled, "That's the way it is. What do you mean?"

So, when the school explained that Waya and his family lived off the grid for several years, I could understand their motivation. I also understood that Waya was not operating off the same set of expectations as other kids on the reservation. Opportunistic and cunning, Waya tried to escape every time they brought his lunch each day. As we stood outside his padded classroom, the educator first warned me, "If you even crack this door a little. He will run, and we will spend so much time just trying to get him. Talk to him through the door." I peeked through the small sliver of the reinforced plastic window on the door. Waya stood in the corner with a blank look on his face, waiting to see what would happen.

"Hey, do you care if I hang out in there with you?" I asked. Waya nodded. As the educator unlocked the door, she explained how I would need to turn my body sideways to squeeze inside. I did as instructed, entering at an angle that blocked the door. After one minute in the room, I could tell why Waya was eloping at every chance. The room was small, maybe 8-by-8 feet, lined with nothing but blue padding so he could scream and punch the walls without hurting his hands. I felt disgust and rage standing in that room. I couldn't imagine what this fourth-grade "off-the-grid" child must have been feeling, so I asked. Waya said that he liked the school, but he didn't like the other students in his class. He also hated being in this room, which he had been in most of the year.

At that time, a group of high school mentors came in to work with Waya. I watched their interactions and how Waya lit up as much as the high school mentor. I saw joy between them, subdued by the heaviness of their learning environment.

I knocked on the window to leave the room and process my observations. My first question was, "I want to take him out of this room. Could we try something for 30 minutes?" I saw immediate panic on both of the educators' faces as they quickly rattled off stories of how he had run away at every opportunity. I decided to model to them the power of mutually co-constructed rewards with clear, high expectations. After checking with the assistant principal, I was given the green light to try the intervention.

When the high school mentors left, I went back into the room with Waya for lunch. We sat in the room together to eat and talk. As we ate, he explained how he preferred working with older kids rather than his classmates. I said, "You did amazing with the mentor, and I know you said you want to get out of this room. Want to come up with a plan to do that?" A crooked smile slowly crept across his face as he stopped twirling his mashed potatoes.

I continued, "We can get out of here, but we have to convince the teachers that you won't run away." He then stopped smiling, and his body language became less animated. I continued, "The thing is, Waya, if we say we aren't going to run away, but then we do, they might not trust you as quickly next time. I'm only here for two more days, and I'd love to help you not be in this room anymore."

Waya and I then practiced how to talk to the educators: to ask permission to leave, explain what he would do if he had the urge to run away (focus on something blue to remind him of the room), and plan what he would do if allowed to leave the room. He successfully communicated that to the educator as I sat cross-legged in the small room with him. I let him leave the room first, following behind him. Waya immediately walked over to a designated desk about 10 feet from the door of the room to begin working on an assignment.

Waya had not had many successful days outside the blue room, but this day was his breakthrough. The way things have always been done is not always the best or the way it has to be. This is a clear example of how we can rethink discipline to get better results. We understood the driver of the behavior: a desire to escape and a lack of fitting in with peers. We addressed this with replacement skills and intrinsic motivation to challenge him, and Waya, like kids all around the world, with this approach, rose to the occasion and was successful.

The Challenge: Punitive Discipline Is Hurting Us All

My first international speaking event was in Brussels in 2017, where I presented my framework for implementing restorative discipline in schools. One gentleman in the audience asked question after question throughout my presentation—so many that I began to wonder if I had gotten something wrong. To my surprise, he came up afterward, shook my hand, and said that he admired my approach to school discipline. It turned out this man was Terry O'Connell, someone I had cited many times in my slides.

Terry was an Australian police sergeant and a pioneer in adapting and formalizing restorative justice within policing. In 1991, he created the Wagga Wagga Police restorative conference script and a set of restorative questions to address youth crime, later expanding this model into communities, schools, and workplaces. The last thing this 30-year veteran police officer said to me before walking away was, "I think we will heal the world through schools a lot quicker than through prisons and police."

I, too, believe deeply that restorative practices reveal a powerful path to interrupt cycles of harm and that lasting peace begins in the classroom. When we start at the root—with our students—we can see it ripple outward into communities, across states, and even globally.

I have seen the impact of restorative practices within our schools firsthand, having worked in more than two dozen countries and in almost every state in the United States. I have collaborated with researchers, government entities, and universities and implemented the strategies within this book directly into some of the most complex school environments with the highest violence rates around the world. I understand how intentional implementation, wrap around supports, and accountability loops can transform school systems.

Restorative practices can help reimagine our approach to discipline. We need a model that doesn't rely on fear and shame but instead heals, sustains accountability, and addresses the root causes of behavior with empathy and logic. Punitive discipline not only fails to create lasting change—it harms our students, teachers, parents, and everyone involved by fracturing relationships and undermining accountability. The tools you will find in this book will build and transform your approach to discipline, ideally professionally and personally. It is about shifting the way you approach the same problems with different strategies that increase learning and improve communication.

Every educator has faced a hair-pulling moment: a classroom disruption that halts your perfectly planned lesson. All eyes turn to you, waiting to see how you'll handle it. Traditionally, we've reached for the quick fixes—sending students to the office, assigning detentions, or even using fear or shame to make the behavior stop. Sure, it feels like you're taking control when you do one of those things, but let's be honest, how often does it actually stop the negative behavior from continuing to happen in the future? What's your "return on investment" for doing the traditional discipline?

Punitive discipline doesn't correct behavior in the long run because it relies on fear as its primary motivator. Fear may generate short-term compliance, but when the motivator of fear goes away, the consequence is no longer effective and often makes things worse. Fear can quickly shift to anxiety, break down connections, and cause kids to become desensitized as a way to cope.

When we give consequences that don't match the root causes of a student's behavior, we often cause unintended harm: pain, embarrassment, or shame. These feelings come up when a student has not been given the dignity to make things right—something restorative practices support. These outdated practices cost schools time and resources, strain teachers' mental well-being, and can seriously impact a child's long-term outcomes. Punishment alone doesn't teach skill replacement or develop the prosocial behaviors we want to see more of. Fear-driven approaches also shut down the very things students need to grow: vulnerability, trust, and connection. In some cases, they rely on exclusion that leads to ostracizing students who are already struggling, leaving them unsure how to connect to their community or form meaningful relationships.

If we want to be an embodied practitioner of the strategies in this book, we have to understand the science behind discipline, find proactive and responsive tools to implement, and establish the quality of space. When we discipline students traditionally, we sometimes miss the chance to teach them about accountability and empathy. Traditional methods often lead to resentment and repeated misbehavior. But when we shift to restorative practices, we open the door to understanding them, fixing things, and growing stronger relationships.

This change isn't just about handling disruptions better—it's about creating an environment where every student feels a sense of belonging and is given opportunities to repair harm due to valuing their community. And it begins with first seeking to understand the drivers behind a behavior. But, before we unpack this first strategy, let's take a deeper look into the science behind the top three reasons we must move away from punitive discipline.

Shifting from Control to Connection

For decades, school discipline systems have relied on external motivators like punishments or rewards to enforce compliance. But as our understanding of human behavior and motivation has evolved, it's become increasingly clear: these approaches often backfire. They may silence negative behavior temporarily, but they rarely lead to lasting growth, empathy, or self-awareness. This is because not all types of motivation are created equal.

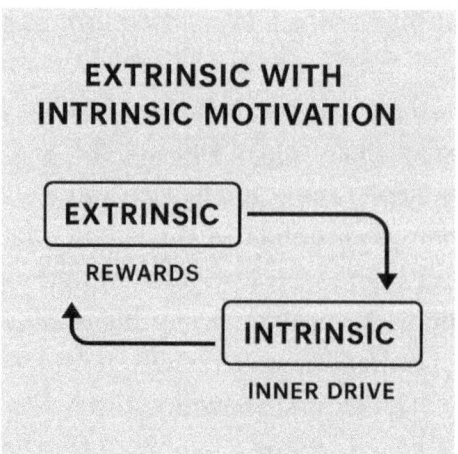

To build schools where students thrive, not just comply, we must understand the science behind what truly motivates people, and the difference between extrinsic and intrinsic motivation. When we discipline from a place of control, we suppress students' ability to self-regulate, reflect to self-correct, and even grow. When we create systems that feed internal passions and motivation, we can build communities where students take ownership of their actions and feel a sense of belonging and purpose.

When a student follows a rule to avoid punishment, rather than valuing or respecting the reason behind a rule, this is **extrinsic motivation**. Motivation that is dependent on painful consequences often evokes emotions associated with fear. We know that fear can cause feelings of helplessness, dysregulation, anger, sadness, isolation, and several other negative emotions. This type of motivation also uses rewards to motivate us, such as:

- Positive grades
- Positive accolades
- Positive notes/calls home
- Candy, extra privileges, and other things you can "win"

Intrinsic motivation arises when we engage in behaviors that spark joy, curiosity, or a sense of purpose—making us want to repeat that activity or behavior for its own sake, rather than for external rewards or fear of consequences. The feelings behind intrinsic motivation are often connected to a sense of fulfillment. These emotions support a deeper and more lasting form of motivation that is empowering rather than controlling.

This motivation is driven by internal rewards such as:

- A sense of accomplishment
- Enjoyment of the task itself
- Personal interest or curiosity
- Desire to improve or master a skill
- Feeling aligned with personal values or purpose
- Emotional satisfaction from helping others or contributing to something meaningful

Research by Edward Deci and Richard Ryan (Self-Determination Theory) shows that *extrinsic motivators like punishment actually suppress intrinsic motivation*, reducing curiosity, creativity, and authentic engagement. Instead of building self-regulation, it creates fear-driven compliance. A student repeatedly sent to detention for talking out of turn might stop participating altogether—not because they've learned respect but because they fear the punishment. They internalize the message: *Stay silent, don't be yourself.*

Students in zero-tolerance schools often show higher dropout rates and lower test scores, not better behavior (American Psychological Association Task Force, 2008). One compelling body of evidence comes from a study referenced in *Drive* by Daniel Pink. The same researchers from the Self-Determination Theory also found that when institutions like schools, families, sports teams, or businesses use external rewards and punishments to control behavior, they inadvertently undermine intrinsic motivation. To be clear, the more we try to manage people's behavior through power and consequences, the less ownership the other person feels over their choices and the less likely they are to grow into self-regulating, empathetic individuals.

Discipline systems rooted in control often miss the deeper goal of helping people *understand* their actions and *repair* harm. We need a shift from compliance to a focus on growth, from punitive consequences to relational accountability, and from kids feeling helpless to feeling empowered to make things right.

If we want students to develop empathy, self-awareness, and responsibility, our discipline practices must reflect those values. We can't afford to confuse momentary compliance or obedience with real behavioral shifts. This book will go over strategies to bring intrinsic motivation into your discipline practices and classroom management.

Fear-Based Discipline Desensitizes Kids

I still remember, as a kid, what it felt like to be yelled at, to have things taken away without explanation, and being ordered to do something for no other reason than "because I said so." Consequences were handed down quickly, meant to punish, not to teach me a better, more meaningful way to do something. They were rooted in fear.

Eventually, I stopped caring. Not just about the rules but even about myself and others. I felt dangerously numb. I was a pre-teen carrying weapons, living in constant survival mode, desensitized to the consequences that were meant to "keep me in line."

At its worst, fear-based discipline asks kids to follow rules that are arbitrary or even cruel, causing them to shut down emotionally. It doesn't teach; it controls. And when control is the goal, compliance becomes the only way to win . . . but at what cost?

My theory: Fear kills curiosity, smothers empathy, and stifles the sparks of passion a kid might be developing. Obedience may keep things quiet in the short term, but the research also shows it blocks the release of dopamine and oxytocin, the chemicals that help kids feel connected, happy, and confident!

When we raise kids on obedience instead of exploration and growth, we're not building thinkers. We're training followers. We're not teaching emotional intelligence—we're suppressing it. And we've known this for a long time. Even back in 1991, a study by Baumrind found that kids raised under authoritarian parenting styles were more likely to struggle with anxiety, depression, and resentment toward authority throughout their lives. So, if we know this, why are we still choosing fear over understanding?

Punitive Discipline Doesn't Support Conflict Resolution Skills and Learning

When punitive discipline happens, students are often removed from the conflict rather than invited to learn through it. A student gets suspended or sent out of class, and suddenly, the opportunity to teach conflict resolution is gone. The problem might be paused, but nothing has really been solved—and certainly nothing has been taught.

We can't expect students to navigate conflict better in the future if we haven't taught them the skills to do so. And punitive consequences don't teach replacement behaviors; they are quick and standardized.

When I was working in residential care, I learned that if I didn't teach through a logical consequence the behavior would typically happen again. Working directly on the violent offender unit, I saw students who didn't fear consequences. Fear would trigger them more but logical accountability felt safe and a problem they could solve instead of having something just done to them. I found that when I unpacked with them how their behavior caused harm and involved them in a plan to repair it, the kids showed a stronger sense of accountability and commitment to change.

Neuroscience backs up why this happens. In *The Whole-Brain Child*, neuropsychiatrist Daniel J. Siegel and parenting expert Tina Payne Bryson explain how shame and fear light up the brain's fight/flight system, impairing memory, problem-solving, and emotional regulation. In contrast, emotionally safe learning environments activate the prefrontal cortex—the part of the brain responsible for decision-making and empathy. This shows me that we can't teach empathy if we do it using fear-based approaches.

As Dr. Brené Brown's research shows, vulnerability is the birth-place of learning, growth, and connection. But when students are punished into silence, they lose the chance to practice that vulner-ability, just when they need it most. Instead of shutting kids down, we need to help them understand the driver behind their behavior, how to build back trust, and give them chances to repair harm.

The Strategy: Understanding What's Behind the Behavior

All behavior is a form of communication. When students act out, they are telling us something—maybe they are bored, frustrated, sad, or struggling at home. Our job as educators is to become behavior detectives to uncover the underlying drivers or triggers for why the behavior occurred when it did.

This is always the starting point for using restorative practices.

So, what could be driving the behavior? There are often three fundamental reasons kids act out: power and autonomy struggles, skills deficits (emotional, academic, or social), and/or unmet needs (emotional or physiological).

Power and autonomy struggles: Kids crave a sense of control, especially in systems where they feel powerless. Acting out becomes a way to:

- Assert independence
- Push back against authority
- Regain a sense of agency after feeling helpless or overlooked

A power struggle might look like asking a student to stop texting in class and receiving a flat "No." You lock eyes, fold your arms, and respond, "Put away your cell phone right now," standing there waiting for them to comply. With other students watching as you assert your dominance, the student may try to "save face" and push back more. This type of assertive reaction can also sometimes create an amygdala response—a fight, flight, or freeze state. Adults and kids both want peace and a sense of control. When we respond with calm, assertive redirection, without adding additional pressure or shame, we allow the student to hear us more clearly.

Restorative practices help create a fair, balanced power dynamic between adults and students by giving kids a sense of voice and control in how situations are handled. Instead of demanding compliance, we should redirect with a brain-aligned strategy by offering two choices. For example, you might say, "You can either put the phone away, or I'll need to decide what happens next. I'll give you a minute to think about it." Then step away. When we present them with just two ideas, we can move the thinking from the amygdala to the prefrontal cortex, ideally, allowing room for a good decision to be made.

That moment of space matters a lot—it gives the student a chance to pause, reflect, and choose without pressure. One option allows them to meet the expectation and keep their power (by putting the phone away without taking further action). The other carries a consequence, but because it wasn't spelled out, it avoids the common trap where students weigh whether the consequence is "worth it." This subtle shift preserves student dignity, reinforces expectations, and gives them real-time practice in making thoughtful decisions.

If they choose not to put away the cell phone in the one-minute redirection time, that's when we implement a logical consequence.

Also, it's important to realize that sometimes, what might seem like a power struggle is actually a student trying to test the boundaries, fulfill an underlying need for autonomy, or gain control when they are feeling fear or anxiety. So, it's important to use standardized ways to redirect that help us to check any bias we may have and see the situation clearly for what it is.

Skills deficits: A lot of behaviors that we label as "defiance" are actually signs of deficits in the following areas:

- **Emotional regulation,** including difficulty managing frustration.
- **Executive functioning,** more common with ADHD, autism, and trauma survivors.
- **Communication,** most often with students acting out to divert attention away from academic struggles, from fear of being seen as behind.

When students are missing key social, emotional, or behavioral skills, those gaps often show up as "attention-seeking behaviors." But what if we looked at these not as problems to be punished but as a message to be read? In many cases, these are actually connection-seeking behaviors—a student's way of saying, "I don't know how to get my needs met, but I need someone to notice me."

Students rarely say, "I need help" or "I want to feel seen." Instead, they more often act out, interrupt, or challenge expectations—not to be difficult but because they're missing the skills to connect in more appropriate ways.

When kids don't know how to communicate the connection they need, they behave in ways that demand it. For example, a student who throws a pencil across the room might really be saying, "Please see me. I feel invisible," or "I want people to like me in class, I don't know how to fit in." Connection-seeking behaviors can look like interrupting or ignoring, yelling in class, eye-rolling, physical aggression, destroying items, running away, lying, and exaggerating.

When we respond to those behaviors with punishment or harsh correction, we often miss the root cause: the skill deficit. Even our tone or body language can unintentionally feed the behavior by reinforcing the student's belief that the only way to get attention is through disruption.

Instead, a more effective and compassionate approach is to quietly redirect without shaming, and just as importantly, proactively give positive attention when the student is meeting expectations. This builds connection and reinforces the very skills they're missing.

Connection-seeking behaviors often signal an unmet need or lagging skill. If we shift our lens from punishment to skill-building, we don't just manage behavior—we train it.

Unmet needs: Sometimes our students may not have eaten that morning, or even in a couple of days. Sometimes they may not have slept the night before, or they have family issues preventing them from going home. There are many reasons why our students may be acting out, but unmet needs are often the base for a student not feeling regulated. We can try to guess the unmet needs, but the best way to identify them is through a solid relationship. When you have a relationship with a student, they can feel comfortable sharing good things as well as challenges.

Neuroscience shows that trauma rewires children's brains into survival mode quicker than normal. More than 50 years of research confirms strong links to delayed emotional processing, instability, stress responses, and atypical neural development. Experiences of maltreatment have been shown to impact multiple brain structures. Healing happens by teaching the brain new patterns and understanding that developing executive functioning skills can build stronger pathways to improve in areas where deficits exist.

What does that look like in the classroom? It might be the kid who explodes over a pencil falling on the floor and breaking. Or the one who refuses to follow directions—not because they're "defiant" but because their brain is constantly wired for danger, and your redirection might trigger something that makes them feel insecure.

These behaviors aren't problems to fix; they're signals showing us where training is needed. They're the brain's way of saying, "Something is wrong, and I don't have the skills to handle it." Or it might be the need for safety, for belonging, for understanding, or just someone to ask, "What's going on?" instead of "What's wrong with you?"

To address this, schools need to shift from being compliance-driven to needs-responsive and curious. That means training staff in trauma-informed strategies, restorative practices, creating systems that prioritize relationships, and giving students access to emotional support.

How to Guide: Discipline That Seeks to Understand

Let's break down the steps to implementing these strategies in your classroom.

Step 1: Identify the Behavior

Start by observing and documenting the behavior. You can even document the situation, frequency of behavior, possible triggers, and patterns. This helps you understand the bigger picture and identify and know how quickly you should intervene.

A simple way to quickly think about what discipline action you need to take starts with looking through the three drivers we've talked about. Is it an unmet need, a skill deficit, or a desire for connection or personal sense of power?

Ask yourself questions like:

- *Is this student struggling with something academic or social?*
- *Could this be a connection-seeking behavior that just doesn't come out in the most helpful way?*
- *Do I sense a power struggle forming, or are they craving some autonomy?*

When we pause, regulate, and reflect on patterns like this, we start to create a blueprint for how we should engage. That gives us insight to support the student, instead of just reacting to what we see or feel on the surface. It's not about having all the answers. Sometimes it's just about knowing which questions to ask ourselves first.

Step 2: Use Active Listening

Active listening is seriously a secret weapon. When a student misbehaves, engage with the student in a nonconfrontational conversation and take a moment to truly listen to their side of the story. Ask open-ended questions like:

- "What happened?"
- "What's going on?"

- "What were you feeling at the time?"
- "What do you need right now?"
- "What could we do differently next time?"

This shows you care to learn about their perspective first before judging with a response.

Active listening is about noticing the emotions and feelings behind the words. Students can feel the difference when we listen to truly try to understand them, and they're more likely to open up and engage in the process of finding a solution when they feel that you sincerely care. It builds trust and mutual respect, making students more open to your guidance.

Take the time to build a relationship with students through listening. Show genuine interest in their well-being and make it clear that you're there to help. Understanding the why behind the behavior is crucial for finding effective ways for them to be successful long-term.

Step 3: Set Expectations, Reflect, and Build a Plan Together

Accountability can be a learning opportunity if we allow students to be active participants in the discipline process. We can teach kids that they have the ability to maintain their sense of power if they follow expectations. One way to do this is by co-constructing alignments to make sure you are both on the same page about what happened with a plan for repair, if needed.

Empower your students by involving them in finding solutions to their problems. When students have a say in how to make things right, they're more likely to take ownership of their actions. Ask them, "What do you think needs to happen to fix this?" Then guide them toward constructive solutions.

Involving students in the problem-solving process helps them develop critical thinking and decision-making skills. It also reinforces the idea that they have the power to make positive changes. When students are part of the solution, they're also more invested in the outcome and more likely to follow through.

Create a plan for repairing the harm together. Ensure the plan is clear, specific, actionable, and time-bound. This might include written or spoken apologies, restitution, community service, or helping out in the classroom. The key is to make the consequence meaningful and related to the behavior. The plan should also be realistic and achievable, with specific deadlines to ensure accountability. By doing this, you build dignity through active accountability, responsibility to fix things, and a path to growth. This is a process that builds trust and emotional intelligence.

Step 4: Follow-Through

Monitor the student's progress and provide ongoing support. Check in regularly to see how they're doing and offer guidance as needed. Revisit the plan if necessary and acknowledge improvements. This shows the student that you're invested in their growth and success.

Regular follow-ups demonstrate that you care about the student's development and are committed to helping them succeed. It's also important to celebrate their progress and provide constructive feedback to keep them on track. This ongoing support reinforces the positive changes and helps prevent future misbehavior.

What Could Go Wrong?

When we react to student behavior from a place of frustration or urgency, we risk escalating the situation. A raised voice, sharp tone, or visible annoyance, even if unintentional, can trigger a student's stress response, especially for those with trauma histories. Rather than calming the moment, we may fuel dysregulation. The opportunity to build trust, model emotional regulation, and teach skills goes away. Without a calm and restorative response, discipline becomes something we *do to* students, rather than something we build *with* them. Our regulation is key.

This is why, before we can get to the root of the driver of a behavior, we must take a moment to make sure we are calm. As Dr. Bruce Perry says, "A dysregulated adult can never regulate a dysregulated child," in the book he co-authored with Oprah Winfrey, *What Happened to You?: Conversations on Trauma, Resilience, and Healing.*

Stay clear with your words, neutral with your emotions, and calm but assertive with your tone. Take a deep breath, think about your happy place, and redirect with a clear mind. This approach can help de-escalate the conflict and give you more capacity to listen with curiosity.

Staying calm doesn't mean being passive. It means maintaining control of your emotions and responding thoughtfully. You teach more from your actions than your words. Your ability to stay grounded will be an example for students to model, showing them how to handle conflicts. In Chapter 5, we'll explore this further and equip you with strategies for self-regulation and co-regulation.

Once you feel regulated and ready, you can approach the student and show them you are actively listening with these cues:

- **Make eye contact:** Show students you're engaged. Don't force students to make eye contact with you, but do show them you notice them.

- **Nod and provide validation:** Acknowledge understanding. Summarizing and showing you understand the emotions behind their words is crucial.

- **Avoid interrupting:** Let students finish their thoughts. Use open questions to steer the conversation forward.

Scenario: Stay Curious: A Parent Driving Their Son Home After School

Staying curious is the foundation to understanding behavior. Going back to the three major reasons kids may act out, here is an example of how staying curious can help to neutralize power struggles (shifting the dynamic from control to collaboration), create a safe space for connection (invites emotional availability rather than shame), and practice being a behavior detective to uncover unmet needs (asks the *why*, rather than the *what*).

Parent (Using Open-Ended Questions and Affirmations):

"Hey, I've noticed you seem kind of off lately—like you've got a lot on your mind. You're usually bouncing around and love to talk with me, but lately, you seem quieter. I can see it at school, and even with chores at home. What's going on?"

(Instead of asking "Why are you acting like this?" which can feel accusatory, this approach observes behavior without judgment and invites the child to talk.)

Son (Shrugs, Avoidant):

"I dunno. Nothing's wrong."

Parent (Reflective Listening and Normalizing Feelings):

"Hmm. Yeah, I get that. Sometimes I don't even know why I feel off either. But I can tell something' is weighing on you. I wonder if it's something around school or home that is feeling kind of frustrating lately?"

(Here, the parent reflects back what they're seeing while also leaving space for the child to clarify.)

Son (Small Admission, Still Deflecting):

"School's fine. It's just boring."

Parent (Rolling with Resistance and Expanding the Conversation):

*"Boring? I feel you. Sitting still all day, dealing with assignments . . . .
I struggled when I was a kid, Bro. Is there something at home that
I could help you with or that you want to vent about?"*

(Instead of contradicting or pushing back, the parent goes with the child's response and asks a nonthreatening follow-up question.)

Son (Opens Up a Little More):

*"I don't know. I just hate having to drive so far. It takes us 50 minutes
to get to school every morning and then another 50 minutes to get
home. I wish you lived closer to Mom."*

Parent (Validating and Evoking Change):

*"Yeah. I understand that it is so boring being stuck in a car that long
every morning and evening when you're with me. I know we want to
move closer, but I need to save up a bit longer before I can move. Since
we can't really change the drive, since you love seeing me and want to
go to the same school you go to now, how about we come up with something fun we can do every car ride?"*

(The parent acknowledges emotions rather than dismissing them and helps the child start thinking about ways to take action.)

Son (Starting to Reflect):

"Yeah. I guess. But I don't know what."

Parent (Empowering and Problem-Solving Together):

"It's tough to come up with something on the spot. Let's brainstorm together, but I want you to know I love you and understand this drive sucks, Bro. If anything, though, is ever on your mind outside of just the drive, know you can come to me with anything, and we will always decide how to respond with what you tell me together."

(Now, the parent shifts toward empowerment, making the child an active participant in the solution or understanding that future support is available.)

Why This Works:

No interrogation, no pressure: Just a laid-back or low-stakes conversation.

Open-ended questions: Instead of "Are you okay?" (which invites a shutdown "Yeah, I'm fine"), the questions are more curious and go with the flow of the conversation naturally.

Reflective listening: The parent repeats back what they hear, showing understanding without judgment.

Normalizes feelings, uses directness, and humor: Acknowledging the frustration makes the child feel less alone, which keeps their mind open to understanding. When someone is struggling, being direct and light-hearted goes a long way. It signals compassion in your interaction, which helps to naturally de-escalate interactions with others.

Rolls with resistance: The parent doesn't push; *they follow the child's lead* and guide them toward self-discovery.

Encouraging the child to problem-solve: Instead of *telling* the child what to do, they give them autonomy by *evoking* personal or collaborative solution development. Keeping the child in control of the conversation helps keep it moving forward.

Parent Huddle

It Takes a Village: The Power of the Parent Huddle

Kids don't just grow up in classrooms. They grow up in kitchens, on couches, in cars, with friends, online, and in interactions happening long after the last school bell rings. If we really want to build consistent, meaningful change in how we approach behavior, we have to include families as part of the team. That's where the *parent huddle* comes in.

Parent huddles offer parents an opportunity to learn and use similar strategies we are using in school at home; it's a consistency bridge. They are a way to share one simple, easy-to-implement discipline strategy at a time that matches classroom discipline. Parents often want to help but may feel unsure how to respond when their child is acting out or struggling emotionally. This gives us an easy "start here" point for them by helping create consistency in one strategy instead of just a list of ones to try.

If you're a parent yourself, you can bring these strategies home and model them in your own family life. If you're an educator, you can coach parents gently and respectfully, sharing what's worked and walking alongside them as they build new skills, too, with this consistency bridge. This parent huddle is about creating a safe space for sharing and active listening.

Hold Regular Circles at Home Establishing regular family meetings as a circle will help you strengthen relationships at home, prepare kids with communication skills, and create a proactive structure to help navigate the difficult conversations when they come. Here are the steps:

1. Create a regular time where you can practice a circle with your family.

2. Start with mindfulness, like deep breathing together or pleasant imagery, to center everyone.

3. In the circle, it's best to start by discussing fun and interesting topics. Then you can move into navigating deeper conversations that require vulnerability. Like "What have you been thinking, feeling, or needing after grandma passed away?" If you start immediately with that topic without ever practicing regular family meetings or circles, your kids might not be ready to open up as quickly.

4. Create the expectations that allow everyone to have their voice heard when discussing the topic and what to do if someone doesn't agree.

5. Use a "Talking Piece," which can be something you have at home that is meaningful to everyone. Whoever holds this is the only one who talks at that time in the circle. It creates an easy, fun way to practice active listening and focused attention.

6. Create a closing activity/ritual at the end of the circle to bring a sense of fun (for example, write down a shared goal for the week or listen to a favorite song together).

The power of this activity is that you are modeling healthy communication and giving your family a regular outlet to be heard. If we continue to build structures that are protective and teaching in the home, I believe we will see more thriving students in the classroom.

2

Building Belonging

Discipline That Doesn't Create Shame, Fear, or Embarrassment

"Don't let the world define who you are. You are the only person who has that power."

—Sinéad O'Connor

Seek to Understand: Why Belonging Matters

In elementary school, I was labeled as the "bad kid," a reputation that followed me through middle school. I felt constant pressure to "act right" and "behave." But the more I conformed to blend in, the more anger built inside me, and with it a growing sense of isolation. This anger began to come out in explosive ways—I punched holes in walls, ran away, and had massive outbursts.

My parents and teachers responded with harsher punishment, which only fueled the fire.

Belonging never felt real for me. Even to this day, I still wrestle with feelings of not fitting in. At the same time, this struggle has also enabled me to be a good teacher of this work, navigate difficult conversations, and help others see things they might have overlooked. It has helped me deepen others' understanding of how the search for belonging shapes us all.

The story I am about to share with you is about a young man named Orion who took his own life. If you are sensitive to this topic, please skip to the "Challenge" section.

It's believed that Orion didn't feel like he fit in or belonged for several personal reasons that I have chosen not to share in this book in order not to glorify, glamorize, or demonize his story. He wrote letters to several of his friends in school and then committed the act of violence on himself, devastating his family, friends, teachers, classmates, and the community. I offered to help the community heal through a healing circle, a type of circle that I created to help people to process deeply harmful situations.

Orion was an artist, so we used a paintbrush—gifted by the muralist who was painting a tribute in his honor for his family—as our talking piece. The talking piece is not just an object you bring to a circle; it's a symbol of trust, dignity, and belonging. When someone holds the talking piece, the entire room listens, not to respond, not to interrupt, but to truly hear the person and their intentions. It ensures that every voice, no matter who you are, carries the same weight and worth as every other person. It centers our attention and reminds us that healing starts with listening to *understand*. In that moment, with the talking piece in hand, we are saying: you matter, your story matters, and we are here for all of it.

I opened the circle by introducing myself and outlining the expectations and goals of the circle: to heal and build structures of support for everyone directly involved. I then modeled and facilitated a calming, pleasant imagery activity with deep breathing. Once the group was centered, I slowly guided them through a series of prompts that I had written, switching between questions that invited different levels of vulnerability. I asked them to share both happy memories of Orion and the toughest parts about losing him and his absence in their lives.

The entire group had the opportunity to speak or just listen. The school administrator who joined us in the healing circle was also personally affected by the loss of a family member to suicide during his childhood. His presence was a beacon of hope to everyone in the group and a reminder that sharing our stories has power and can make others feel less alone. After the circle, a mother came up to me and said that her son hadn't spoken about the situation since it happened and refused to talk to a therapist. She was deeply concerned that he might blame himself or even be experiencing the same thoughts and feelings as Orion. Yet in the circle, even after just losing his best friend, he opened up in ways she'd never seen before.

As a group, we co-created a simple yet powerful action item to help prevent this kind of devastating loss in the future: to make everyone feel like they belong, to support each other, and to pay attention to the signs when someone might feel like they don't. Lastly, we decided everyone needed to get a blue slushy at the gas station on the corner in remembrance of Orion. This was something he would do after school with his younger sisters and was a way for everyone to celebrate his life.

As someone who had a suicide attempt when I was 13, I personally know what it's like to feel overwhelmingly alone, with no one to turn to or to help process heavy emotions.

I created the healing circle process to help people unpack their emotions with structure and support, especially the complex feelings that might feel stuck or difficult to share. Healing circles are also a proactive way to help prevent further loss and harm, building micro-communities that serve as a protective factor for everyone involved. Sometimes it takes only one person to notice when someone is struggling to make a difference.

The Challenge: Shame Pushes Away Belonging

Many people confuse shame with guilt, yet they play very different roles in discipline and in shaping our sense of belonging. Shame is a painful emotion that typically comes from believing we've done something others, or we ourselves, see as wrong, improper, or dishonorable. When kids experience this often in life, it can become tied to their sense of self. Brené Brown, a leading researcher on shame, defines it as "the intensely painful feeling or experience of believing that we are flawed and therefore unworthy of love and belonging." Guilt, on the other hand, is related to a specific behavior that leaves the door open to "fix" something.

- **Guilt** says, "I did something bad." Guilt is a healthy emotion rooted in empathy and recognizing the harm we've done and the effects of our behavior. It motivates us to take constructive action and accountability.

- **Shame** says, "I am bad." Shame is an emotion that causes us to feel fear and is what punitive discipline thrives on. It makes us feel helpless to change the situation and causes us to turn inward to protect ourselves. It can cause us to withdraw from others and is detrimental to our sense of belonging.

In the classroom, shame can come from being publicly disciplined, excluded without conversation, or made to feel "less than." It can deeply damage a student's sense of identity. Take, for example, something like Positive Behavior Intervention and Supports (PBIS), which publicly tracks students' points. Even with good intentions, these systems can promote comparison, competition, and exclusion, leading to shame. When these systems are displayed for the entire class to see, like clip charts or posting every student's points on a screen, they are especially harmful for neurodivergent students and those who struggle with regulation. The message this sends is: you are different, and your "failures" are public, where you can't fix them. Over time, this can reinforce a harmful self-view. The student starts to think of themselves as "I'm bad" instead of "I need help with . . . ."

Shame also can creep in when a student is embarrassed in front of their peers after a "roast" goes too far, after a name is called wrong and someone laughs, or even when a punishment is given without conversation. These are all things that show a student they are not safe. Not emotionally safe. Not socially safe. Not safe to be themselves in this classroom.

I have also seen countless educators use shame as an "old-school" tool to control behavior, instilling students with a fear of being called out publicly. Shame-based discipline doesn't correct behavior. It brands students. It says, "*You* are the problem." Not "you're having a hard time," not "let's figure this out," but *you, your feelings, your needs, your very presence here—is too much.* These are some of the exact feelings I had as a kid, causing me to explode or be completely noncompliant.

Even after an educator stops using shame as a tool, the harm is often long-lasting. Students may start to view all educators as "the same," feeling fearful around teachers and expecting to be misunderstood, rather than hoping to experience admiration, curiosity, or connection.

You can see the side effects of shame in the way students flinch when their name is called. The way they stop raising their hand. Stop making eye contact or smiling when they walk into class. The way a student who once wrote poetry now stares at their shoes all class. This is not because they're bad but because somewhere along the line, someone gave them the message that being themselves wasn't okay. Belonging and community can heal this harm, and we can take active steps to support this process with the strategies I'll share in this chapter.

These become experiences that rewire the brain. According to neuroscience, the amygdala—the brain's threat indicator—can't tell the difference between a lion and a teacher who embarrasses them. This is what psychologists call "amygdala hijack." Shame sends students into fight, flight, or freeze. They don't learn from shame. They *respond* to it. And when we use it again and again, we create students who disconnect completely with themselves to comply out of fear or students who start to do the same thing with others, perpetuating a cycle of harm. These aren't isolated moments. They're the results of systems that punish vulnerability instead of protecting it by a sole decision-maker: one teacher in a classroom.

If we trace the word *discipline* back to its roots, it was never meant to punish. It is a tool to teach. It comes from the Latin word *disciplina*, which means instruction or teaching. At its core, discipline was never meant to be about control but about creating **opportunities to fix and improve**.

So, if we are truly disciplining students, every disciplinary moment is also an opportunity for discipleship. Not religious, but relational. Not obedience but *learning together* with mutual accountability around repairing harm.

And when we discipline with shame, we teach kids to see themselves as failures. When we lead with curiosity and connection, we teach them to see themselves as capable of making mistakes and seeking forgiveness. We can help them learn to discern: *Who am I really, even when I mess up? How do I come back from this? Who still stands with me when I fail?*

That's discipline. That's discernment. That's how we build not just better classrooms but more compassionate humans.

The Strategy: Building Belonging Without Shame

What I have learned after visiting schools around the world is that the best classrooms are always those where students and staff prioritize and foster a sense of belonging.

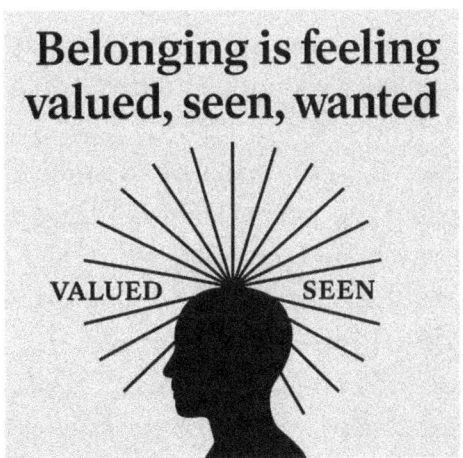

Belonging is feeling valued, seen, and wanted. It is a fundamental core feeling in order to be vulnerable. If we want classrooms to be a place of learning and we know learning happens from failure and trying, we need vulnerability in the classroom. So we must focus on making sure students feel wanted, seen, and valued every time they are around us.

Current data trends also clearly show why this is so vital. According to a report by the Centers for Disease Control and Prevention (CDC), students who feel connected to their school are less likely to engage in risky behaviors, experience mental health issues, or drop out of school. Professor Dacher Keltner's research at UC Berkeley further supports these findings. His studies show that belonging is not just a "nice to have" but a critical factor in student success. Students with a strong sense of belonging are:

- 4.5 times more likely to be *academically motivated*.
- 5.4 times more likely to have *high self-esteem*.
- 3.7 times more likely to *feel hopeful about their future*.

Building belonging in a classroom, as a complex microcommunity, isn't an easy task. And while you can't always predict how your students will show up, the one thing you have control over is how emotionally grounded you are. Belonging begins by making students feel safe and comfortable around you, which they learn by observing how you interact in different situations. As a kid, I remember that the adults I felt the safest around were the ones who I saw handle stressful situations with composure and who managed their anxiety. If they lost their cool, this signaled to me that this person was "not safe."

This is why I teach educators through professional development that the first essential step in building belonging is staying regulated yourself. Managing your stress and anxiety. Managing how you handle conflict. Once students see you navigate a tough situation, it will build trust and teach them how to navigate tough situations too.

We also have to ensure that we are supporting our marginalized students, who may not have the same comfort level in showing vulnerability that other students do. I define marginalized simply as the opposite of the majority. This could be a ratio of gender, race/ethnicity, disability, age, and cognitive levels. Focusing on belonging for the nonmajority is common sense. We can do this through:

- Representation in stories and discussions
- Inclusive activities that allow everyone to have a clear role and equal voice
- Making sure we celebrate differences and have curiosity in the unknown

I strongly believe that when we allow students and adults to be themselves, encourage their intrinsic interests, and respect their autonomy of choice, it creates a freedom of self-expression. And that this expression of self is the key to helping our students find their true passions and career pathways. Creating an environment where students feel safe and free to be themselves, guided by collective expectations that fosters respect and belonging, makes for the ideal learning environment.

How to Guide: Four Ways to Build Belonging and Replace Shame Practices

Imagine walking into your classroom feeling safe, productive, and with calm confidence, not because you have threatened students with harsh consequences but because each student knows they belong and are there to have fun and learn. Their behavior is guided not by fear but by an internal compass that helps them discern how they want to show up and treat others in accordance with their goals and those of the classroom.

Here are four practical strategies any educator can use to create this kind of environment and shift away from discipline that causes shame.

Allow the Student to Feel Heard

What It Is   When a student interrupts your lesson or acts out, instead of calling them out in front of the class, you can ask to speak with them later or take them aside and offer a genuine invitation to discuss the issue without judgment.

Why It Works   Trauma-informed teaching demonstrates that emotional connection soothes the amygdala, which triggers feelings of safety in the student, allowing the thinking brain to re-engage.

Scenario: A Student Cuts You Off While You Are Giving a Lesson   Maya briefly interrupts your lesson by talking with her peers in the back of the classroom. When she does it again, instead of calling her out publicly, you pause, catch her eye, and gesture for her to step aside with you.

You make space for curiosity behind the behavior by asking, "Hey, Maya. That's not normally like you to cut me off when I'm talking. Everything good?"

Maya says, "Ya, sorry."

Teacher says, "Thanks for the apology, it did catch me off guard and made me feel distracted. I think a couple of your peers were also trying to figure out what you were talking about instead of listening to me. Anything you need from me to help you stay on track for the rest of class?"

She says, "No, I'm going to pay attention; sorry I distracted you."

By giving Maya the opportunity to speak and be sincerely heard before discussing how to navigate situations like this better in the future, you avoided triggering shame and built trust by showing her that you were first curious about the situation. If Maya goes back to her seat and talks over you again, this is when you would implement a logical consequence like having her sit next to your desk for the remainder of class or moving her seats away from the peer she has been talking to. It is logical because the consequence aligns with the behavior.

Quick Tip: Practice "Preview, Warning, and Consequence"

The Preview, Warning, and Consequence Model is a trauma-informed and restorative strategy that provides redirection without publicly singling anyone out. Instead of reacting strongly to misbehavior, this model helps slow us down as educators and gives students an opportunity to self-correct their behavior. Predictability in the way we redirect also builds safety for students, helping them know what's coming next when they or a peer is misbehaving.

Step 1: Preview (whole group): Using a calm, steady, and nonthreatening tone, remind students of the co-constructed expectations for the entire class after you see unwanted behavior.

Step 2: Warning (individual): If a student starts to veer off track again and continues negative behavior even after a preview, give a nonescalating, respectful warning—free of blame, shame, or embarrassment. Restate the expectations, without shaming, and let them know that if the behavior continues, a consequence will follow. This warning leaves room for self-correction.

Step 3: Consequence (individual): Follow through with a consistent, logical consequence if the behavior continues. An proportionate consequence is used, not as punishment, but as an opportunity for the student to fix what they are doing wrong and learn. We'll explore logical consequences more in the next chapter. This step is done with compassion and the goal of maintaining the relationship.

Passion Pursuits

What It Is   How often do you allow students to free-think? How much are they encouraged to open up and think about the bigger picture beyond a curriculum, to explore what they enjoy and what interests them? The more we allow students to think freely, the more they will be able to identify what they like and dislike, and the better they will know themselves.

"Passion Pursuits" are intentional, short bursts of unstructured or semistructured time during class where students are encouraged to explore personal interests, ask big questions, or pursue their curiosities unrelated to core content. This could be five minutes of "free-think" journaling, a weekly creative prompt, or a day each month where students build or research something just because it matters to them.

The goal is to shift the learning environment from "task completion" to "exploration," creating space for students to figure out what excites them, what bores them, and how they think when no one is influencing their thoughts. This sends the message that we value their interests and invite them to bring those interests to class, which creates a more inclusive environment, allowing students to be themselves.

Why It Works   When students are given time to think for themselves about something they care about, it reduces stress and increases intrinsic motivation.

Free-thinking time builds the executive functioning muscles students need to self-reflect and problem-solve. As psychologist Mihaly Csikszentmihalyi wrote in his work on *flow*, students are more likely to enter deep learning states when they're immersed in personally meaningful tasks, even if they're not related to a part of the curriculum.

Think of this as classroom permission to wander productively with their minds! Students who know what they love are students who are easier to motivate, because they're not just learning, they're building a meaningful path forward. Intrinsic motivation activities like this are also such a powerful way to build classroom connection. Passion Pursuits are great to do either weekly or daily, depending on the amount of time you have in your schedule. The goal is always just to create a predictable process for your students. The more they understand this is something that they will regularly get to experience with you as an educator, the more vulnerability they will share.

Here are a few examples of passion pursuits you can bring into your classroom:

Friday Wind-Down: "What Sparked You?" Circle (Elementary Classroom)   Gather students in a circle and ask:

"What was one thing this week that made you curious, excited, or happy?"

Students can then share everything from fossils to food, Minecraft to music. This builds community while showing students that *their minds matter*.

Monday Journaling: "What If?" Minute (Middle School English)   Start class by asking students to think openly and creatively:

"What if you could design a school day with only one subject, what would it be and why?"

Students write for three minutes. Some may write about science. Others dream up cooking classes. One student—usually disengaged—fills a page about a Roblox game she wants to build to help people learn how to farm.

Wednesday "Silent Genius Hour" (High School Social Studies) Dedicate 15 minutes a week to Passion Pursuits. Students can read, build, design, sketch, or brainstorm something they are curious about. One group researches the history of streetwear fashion. Another student emails a local activist for an interview. The result? Less resistance, more buy-in during academic lessons because students know they'll also be learning and exploring as individuals.

Offer Group Opportunities to Repair and Grow

What It Is   This strategy turns classroom mistakes, disruptions, conflicts, or even disrespect into meaningful moments of repair and learning. Mistakes always happen in the classroom, but there is a way to make these moments unity-building activities that foster a sense of belonging. Instead of isolating or punishing a student, it involves them in a process that restores relationships and strengthens classroom culture. This might be a student-led apology, a collaborative class check-in, or a joint project that turns harm into healing by teaching our students how to connect with each other.

The focus is on growth and re-connection. Students aren't just forgiven or given a consequence; they're empowered to take responsibility and *actively* repair what was broken, all while being supported in the process.

Why It Works   According to restorative justice principles and the research behind social-emotional learning (SEL), students learn best when they feel safe, connected, and supported.

When students are given the opportunity to repair harm, they move from shame into agency—from "I'm bad" to "I made a mistake, but I can fix it." This builds resilience, empathy, and self-awareness.

The National Education Association found that schools using restorative strategies saw a 44% decrease in suspensions and increased student connectedness. Instead of being labeled as good or bad, students learn to take responsibility for their choices and take actions toward fixing things. Mistakes become opportunities.

Scenario 1: "The Public Apology with a Private Action Plan" (Middle and High School) Jordan shouts a hurtful comment during a peer's presentation, which causes the other student, Tyrone, to become upset and shout back. Instead of sending Jordan or even both students to the office, Mrs. Emery calls for a classroom break and calmly redirects the two students:

"We're going to take a short pause. Work quietly at your desk while preparing for your presentation."

The teacher motions to Tyrone and Jordan to come to her desk for a moment. Mrs. Emery calmly and assertively says:

"I don't know what caused this, but I feel very dysregulated after hearing the yelling and don't appreciate either side of it. Jordan, can you explain to me why you decided to shout at that moment? Yelling was distracting to everyone and was very disrespectful to Tyrone." Jordan suggests apologizing. The option to apologize to Tyrone is also an option that Jordan could come up with himself to show his side of repairing the harm. The teacher calls up Tyrone to her desk; Jordan apologizes, and the other student accepts. Tyrone then heads back to his seat as the teacher talks to Jordan and says, "How can we fix this with the rest of the class?" Jordan says, "I can tell them I'm sorry for shouting out?" The teacher says, "I think that would be a great idea."

Mrs. Emery addresses the class: "We had a brief break, but let's dive back in. Before we do, Jordan wants to say something quickly."

Jordan says, "I shouldn't have shouted out like that and interrupted Tyrone and everyone else, my bad. I won't do that again."

This practice could cause a lot of shame if the teacher forced Jordan to apologize to the class. Since Mrs. Emery asked, "How can we fix it with the rest of the class?" instead of saying "You need to apologize to the class," it put Jordan in the driver's seat to decide how he wanted to resolve the issue with his peers. This created healthy guilt, where he felt empowered and able to fix things.

Typically, I have seen this strategy done quickly at a teacher's desk after a small conflict like this occurs—taking a break, having a quick conversation, and offering a brief ownership and then an apology or action plan between both students. This takes about the same amount of time it takes to call an administrator to come down or fill out a cumbersome referral. Because there is so little time to fill them in on the context, this can lead to a misunderstanding of the conflict, and sometimes, the consequences given do not match the behavior, which takes away from this becoming a teaching moment.

Scenario 2: "The Class Reset Circle" (Elementary)   After a chaotic group activity ends with some arguing and a desk is flipped, a student has to take a timeout outside of the classroom with an adult. Ms. Coleman then gathers the class in a quick circle:

> *"We had a rough moment. Let's take three deep breaths with our eyes closed. Now let's talk for two minutes, meaning each person is allowed to say three to five words each. What can we do to make others feel safe around you?"*

Students brainstorm ideas until the dysregulated student returns to class. It's important for the class to understand how to act inclusively and provide safe actions for a student who may react more quickly or intensely to triggers. In this way, the other students become a buffer, and you are creating connections through their supportive actions, instead of singling out a student whose behavior may already make it hard to build friendships.

Keep Things Fun with "Identity Doodles + Soundtrack Check-In"

Teaching should be fun. These are kids, and the more things are fun and engaging, the more a sense of belonging increases with moments of authenticity and kids expressing themselves. Having "fun" does come with a disclaimer: do not ever use humor at the student's expense. Even light-hearted joking or subtle teasing can become a form of public shaming, undermining the safety you are seeking to create in your classroom.

What It Is   Here is a fast, hybrid creative check-in where you can ask students to express themselves *in the moment* using two forms quickly:

1. A **doodle** (on a sticky note or tablet) representing how they're feeling or something they love right now.
2. A "**class playlist check-in**" each student chooses a song that best describes their mood, energy, or vibe they are currently feeling. They say the song and a brief sentence on why they picked that specific song.

Students can then be prompted or given the choice to share with the class.

Why It Works   It combines:

- **Creative expression** (doodle)
- **Emotional self-awareness** (song/mood pairing)

- **Agency + voice** (choice + spotlight)
- **Neurodivergent accessibility** (nonverbal options)
- **Community micro-bonding** (peer reactions)

And it doesn't take a huge amount of time; it thrives in those *fractured times*. Instead of needing everyone to present, you get spontaneous authenticity *without performative pressure*. It's low-prep, high-impact, and repeatable.

Scenario: Monday, 8:03 a.m. Chaos after late buses and a spill in the cafeteria As students enter, Ms. Chen says, "Doodle how your brain feels right now—don't think, just draw. And if you want to share your 'today's soundtrack,' go ahead and write it on the whiteboard playlist."

Four minutes later, she spins the wheel. It lands on Asher. Asher holds up his doodle—a slinky and a sun. His song? "Skibbidty Toilet."

The class laughs and all snaps (our validation strategy in between people sharing).

"Identity Doodles + Class Playlist Check-In" are quick and easy check-ins—even in chaotic, high-needs classrooms. And best of all? It builds belonging in *real time* using the language kids already speak: self-expression and creativity. It is a simple method that allows students to see their personalities and emotions reflected back to them. Whether used to start the day or reset, it brings fresh energy into the classroom by encouraging students to think, create, and be themselves.

Dos and Don'ts: Replacement Strategies to Stop Outdated Practices

Communication is an amazing tool, especially as educators and parents. We have to understand that kids are sensitive to language and action. They are seeking validation through actions, words, and other means. It's important for us, as one of the adults and models in their life, that we always push not to cause harm with our students. So this section is a quick guide of some of the things we talked about and small shifts in language to avoid pitfalls.

Also, give yourself grace as you're learning, but remember all behavior is a form of communication. It's helpful to listen to students' behavior as a response to your communication. If they react poorly, shift things and adjust. After we make a mistake, it's the best time to repair harm and model a level of vulnerability.

- ☑ **Do** pull students aside privately for tough conversations.
- ☒ **Don't** call them out in front of peers (even with sarcasm).
- ☑ **Do** use open-ended questions like "What was going on?"
- ☒ **Don't** lead with "Why would you do that?" (It triggers defensiveness.)
- ☑ **Do** name the behavior, not the person ("That action hurt someone").
- ☒ **Don't** label the student ("You're always causing problems").
- ☑ **Do** speak in a calm, regulated, and clear tone.
- ☒ **Don't** yell, escalate, or shame with your tone or volume.
- ☑ **Do** give students a chance to repair harm through action.
- ☒ **Don't** isolate or suspend without reflection or restoration.

(continued)

(continued)

- ☑ **Do** use humor *with* students, never *at* them.
- ☒ **Don't** joke about a student's appearance, personality, or mistakes.
- ☑ **Do** validate emotions before redirecting behavior.
- ☒ **Don't** dismiss their feelings with "That's not a big deal."
- ☑ **Do** frame mistakes as learning opportunities.
- ☒ **Don't** make them feel like one mistake defines who they are.
- ☑ **Do** model apology, vulnerability, and emotional intelligence.
- ☒ **Don't** act like you're above correction or too proud to own your impact.
- ☑ **Do** build consistent classroom routines rooted in care and safety.
- ☒ **Don't** rely on behavior charts, public shaming boards, or "good kid" competitions.

What Could Go Wrong

Building a community in the classroom can come with challenges. The following are some common obstacles and strategies to overcome them.

Resistance to Participation

Solution: Start with low-risk activities and gradually increase involvement. These are activities that don't ask the students to discuss vulnerable feelings or tough subjects. You can also pair resistant students with enthusiastic peers to encourage participation.

Action Item: Begin with simple icebreaker games (for example, Identity Doodles and Classroom Playlist Check-In) and slowly introduce more involved activities as students become more comfortable.

Inconsistent Engagement

Solution: Keep activities varied and dynamic. Solicit student feedback to understand what activities they enjoy and find meaningful. I also love to have the students come up with the activities—this creates more intrinsic motivation.

Action Item: Conduct regular surveys or suggestion boxes to gather student input. Adjust activities based on their interests and feedback.

Public Shame Through Punishment

Imagine: You're standing in front of the class, and you call out a student for misbehaving and add a comment that is considered a roast. You were trying to address the behavior quickly and were a bit dysregulated. But here's the problem: public discipline or making a joke at the student's expense often turns into public shaming. Instead of fixing the issue, it leaves students feeling small and embarrassed. Students also usually don't have the opportunity to respond in the classroom setting. You're not just disciplining at this point; you're chipping away at their sense of belonging.

How to fix it: If I notice that I've done this behavior, even if unconsciously, I will bring this up with the student. I admit that I've been reflecting on it and then apologize. I do this especially in situations where I start to feel tension in the relationship and want to understand where it is coming from.

Negative Labeling

Imagine: You called a student a "troublemaker," "lazy," or "disruptive" while trying to discipline them. Suddenly, the focus is not on what they did; it's who they are. These labels are like sticky name tags that don't peel off, and they can have a big impact on their personality. Kids also might start living up (or down) to the labels. These labels can diminish self-esteem and foster the belief that they are inherently flawed or unworthy.

How to fix it: So, what can we do when we've used a label, whether intentionally or not? First, it's important to recognize that the label is a problem, not the kid. Labels like "lazy" or "disruptive" oversimplify what's really going on and fail to address the behaviors or unmet needs behind the actions. Kids aren't inherently bad—they're often struggling with something they can't fully articulate. It might be anxiety, frustration, boredom, or even feeling misunderstood. Instead of labeling them, we need to describe what we're seeing in a way that separates the behavior from their identity.

Let's go through some examples of how we can reframe negative labels into something more constructive:

- **Instead of calling a student "lazy,"** think about what might be driving that behavior. Are they overwhelmed by the task? Are they disengaged because the material doesn't feel relevant to them? Reframe "lazy" as, "You seem unmotivated right now—what's going on? How can I help you get started?" This shifts the focus from judgment to understanding.

- **For a child labeled as "disruptive,"** consider what their actions might be communicating. Are they seeking attention because they feel invisible? Are they testing boundaries because they need a clearer structure? Instead of saying, "You're so disruptive," try something like, "I notice you've been having a hard time staying focused. Is there something you need, or is something bothering you?" This shows them that you're interested in their needs, not just their behavior.

- **A "troublemaker" might be** a kid who feels powerless and is acting out as a way to regain control. Instead of labeling them, address the specific behavior: "Throwing papers isn't okay, but it seems like you're upset about something. Can you tell me what's going on?" This approach acknowledges their feelings while making it clear that their actions have consequences. Then, after we hear the student's side and validate feelings with clear expectations, we can address the driver of the behavior, the control this student might be seeking, "Could you help me hand out some papers to everyone? I know you are really quick at that, and we need to get the class on track again."

Now, here's the big question: Does replacing a negative label with a descriptive one fix the damage done by the first label? The answer is: not completely, but it's a start. Reframing isn't just about finding a new word; it's about actively working to repair the relationship and rebuild the child's sense of self. That means following up with consistent, positive interactions that show the student you see their potential beyond their behavior. It's about helping them rewrite the story they're telling themselves.

For example, if you've accidentally labeled a student as "lazy," you'll need to show them that you believe in their abilities. Praise their efforts when they engage, even in small ways. Remind them that struggle is part of learning and that asking for help doesn't mean they're weak. The goal is to replace the negative self-perception created by the label with a more empowering narrative: "I'm someone who can grow and improve."

At the end of the day, kids aren't just behaviors to manage—they're people to nurture. When we take the time to unpack the reasons behind their actions, we show them that we see them as more than their mistakes. And when we consciously shift away from harmful labels, we create space for them to see themselves in a new light. Changing how we talk about kids—and to kids—doesn't just heal the damage done by labels; it helps prevent that damage in the first place.

The Parent Huddle: Three Ways to Help Your Child Feel Safe, Seen, and Open

Creating a home where your child feels emotionally safe and connected isn't about getting every conversation right or always having the most productive long bonding conversations. It's about choosing connection over correction, curiosity over control, and trust over perfection. This shows them that they belong and are accepted, seen, and valued. Here are three practical, easy ways to help your child open up, especially when it's hard.

Start with Curiosity, Not Correction

When your child comes to you upset, frustrated, or even in trouble, your first instinct might be to fix it—or to get to the bottom of what they "should have done differently." But one of the most effective ways to open communication and avoid shame is to lead with curiosity.

The first step is always to help their nervous system calm down through some sort of regulation activity or pausing the conversation until both you and they are open and ready. Then, instead of jumping into advice, discipline, or questioning them in a way that feels like an interrogation, try to gently wonder with them about what was happening. You can say something like:

> *"That sounds really hard. What do you think was going on for you at that moment?" "I wonder what you may have needed from me or someone else right then? What do you think?"*

This type of questioning shows your child that you're not just trying to manage their behavior—you're trying to *understand them*. It helps them feel seen without feeling judged.

It may take time, and at first, they might give you short answers. That's okay. The key is to be consistent and to mean it when you ask. Your child is more likely to share the big, important stuff if they feel safe sharing the small stuff first.

Let Them Teach You Something About Themselves

Children, especially tweens and teens, often feel like they're constantly being told who to be, how to act, and what they need to fix. One powerful way to reverse that dynamic and build trust is to regularly give them a chance to *teach you* something they care about.

This might look like asking them to show you how to play a game they love, explain a YouTube trend, break down their favorite song lyrics, or walk you through a creative project they're working on. You can say something like:

"I want to know more about what lights you up. Can you show me something you love right now?"

When you do this, you're telling your child: *Your passions matter. You don't have to be impressive to be important here.* This isn't about you understanding the topic perfectly—it's about honoring their voice and their identity. Over time, these moments build confidence and a sense of belonging. When a child feels valued in their natural state, they're more likely to come to you when they're hurting, not just when they're proud.

Apologize and Repair When You Mess Up

We sometimes make mistakes and lose our cool. We say the wrong thing. We misread the moment. What matters most isn't avoiding mistakes; it's how we show up *after* the mistake.

When you've had a hard moment with your child—maybe you raised your voice, dismissed their feelings, or reacted before you listened—make the repair.

You can say: "Hey, I didn't handle that the way I wanted to. I'm sorry. You didn't deserve to feel that way. I want to talk about it in a better way now."

This does a few powerful things. First, it teaches your child that adults aren't above accountability; we're still learning too. Second, it creates a culture of repair. Your child starts to learn that conflict doesn't mean the relationship is broken. And third, it takes shame off the table. Instead of modeling "power over" them (control, force, and hierarchy), you're showing "power with" (collaboration, empathy, and shared responsibility)—which is exactly how trust grows.

These three practices—leading with curiosity, honoring their interests, and modeling repair—can shift the entire emotional climate of your home, allowing your child to open up about something they might be nervous to share. They don't require hours of time or perfect language. They just require you to choose connection in the moment, even when control might feel easier.

Belonging to a Community

Let's make one thing crystal clear: creating a sense of belonging and community in the classroom isn't just beneficial—it's essential.

Imagine a classroom where every student feels valued, respected, and connected. This isn't a distant dream; it's a practical and attainable goal that can profoundly transform the educational experience for our students.

When students feel like they belong, their engagement skyrockets. They participate more, take risks in their learning, and aren't afraid to ask questions or make mistakes. They know they have a safety net of peers and teachers who support them. This sense of belonging fuels their academic performance, turning the classroom into a powerhouse of learning and growth. But it doesn't stop there. The social and emotional benefits are just as profound. Students learn empathy, respect, and collaboration, essential life skills that go far beyond the classroom walls.

It's important for us to create an environment that a student feels safe and seen in. We want to use language and actions that makes our jobs easier and allows students to better understand each other. The more we help students feel like they belong, the more protective factors we are putting into place to help students feel less alone and supported during the hard times. A quick moment of connection with someone can mean everything to them at that time.

This takes effort. It's not a one-and-done task. It requires daily commitment, patience, and a lot of heart. But the rewards are huge. You'll see students who are not just academically competent but emotionally intelligent and socially responsible. You'll witness the joy of students who are excited to come to school, who feel safe to express themselves, and who are eager to support their classmates.

When students know that they are a part of something bigger than themselves, that their presence matters, they rise to the occasion. They become more engaged, more motivated, and more resilient. This is the impact of strong, connected communities. Your classroom can become a supportive space where every student can flourish and an environment where every student has the opportunity to shine.

3

Increasing Accountability

Repairing Harm and Teaching Replacement Skills

"The goal of effective discipline is not to punish but to teach. It's about showing students the consequences of their actions and helping them understand the impact on themselves and others."
—Alfie Kohn, author and educational theorist

Seek to Understand: How the "Toughest" School in NYC Stopped Suspending Students

When I first sat down with Stephanie, I heard her Italian-American New York accent, and it reminded me first of my grandfather, and I could immediately tell two things: she's no nonsense and has a huge heart. Stephanie is the principal at The League School in Brooklyn, New York, where she has worked for more than 48 years. This is the school where students from all five of the New York City boroughs send kids with the most complex needs, including high psychiatric challenges.

She said to me as soon as I sat down, "Nathan, these kids get off the bus . . . ready to go. Ready to fight us, as soon as they get here sometimes off the bus." She continued, "This is their last chance—the last stop. That is what I tell my staff. We have to do something different. We have to help them because there is nothing else past us. And we are the last public school like this across NYC." After her school, these kids have only a few choices left: Department of Corrections, AKA Youth Prison, or psychiatric/residential centers.

NYC is a complex and special place. I knew a lot about the city, as my grandfather grew up in East Harlem in the immigrant public tenements after his family came over from Italy. I knew the grittiness and community that existed here. I also recognized, like with any big change, we'd have to push past some long-standing ways of thinking to make this restorative framework a success. But Stephanie was all in for these kids and was willing to do anything to help them; that's why I was honored she gave my methodology a try.

When we first started talking, we discussed what was working and what was not working. Stephanie shared that her biggest issue was shifting her staff's mindsets about the kids and their behaviors, as well as the inconsistency in how students were being held accountable. In working daily with students who had complicated emotional and behavioral difficulties, her staff struggled with forgiveness and "fresh starts" for the kids. They wanted more effective consequences.

The first thing that Stephnie did to change the culture was to set high expectations with her staff and then with her students.

She looked me in the eyes and said, "I told them, we don't give up on kids here. *Ever.*" I could feel not just her passion but that this was an expectation for everyone in the building. Aligning around that mindset helped the staff understand that when someone is acting out, we have to figure it out, because, as she said, these kids have nowhere else to go. This was the last stop before lockup.

We then focused on implementing the first skill, regulation, for the adults. If the adults stayed regulated, they could co-regulate through their interactions. If they didn't stay regulated around the kids, they would also make the kids dysregulated. So, we taught them coping skills and when to use them. The teachers also took time for breaks through a "tap-in, tap-out" strategy. Lastly, we addressed the lack of fresh starts her staff was willing to give the students after they acted out, and their need for deeper accountability from their students.

Punishment in schools typically helps relieve adults temporarily but rarely teaches the students long term to change their behaviors. *I define punishment as a consequence that doesn't allow someone to have agency over what they did wrong.* I believe consequences are needed for negative harmful behaviors, but I strongly believe that using quick subscribed punishment muffles the curiosity to figure out why the behavior happened. Students start to operate more out of fear, avoidance of the punishment, or lack of caring about the consequence. None of this teaches empathy.

We created structures at The League School to hold students accountable by exploring how their actions affected others and by allowing those impacted to express what they needed to feel safe again and move forward. We also role-modeled situations, practiced ways to better interact, and role-played asking for forgiveness and what that means.

True forgiveness must be expressed in a safe way, so being pressured doesn't work. Outside of owning the behavior through an apology, rebuilding trust comes from more than words. It is seeing those who have caused harm take steps toward making the wrong right. To do this, students need to be given a teaching or logical consequence that helps them learn a lesson. My definition of a *logical consequence* is a consequence to a student's behavior that is directly connected to the reason why they did the harmful action. Rather than punishing, it aims to teach a replacement skill or teach a feeling, building their emotional literacy. If a student destroys a classmate's science project, instead of detention or suspension, they can help rebuild the project to appreciate the effort involved and take part in a restorative conversation to understand how their actions affected their peer.

Because Stephanie set an expectation that "we never give up on kids," one of the most important parts of this process was improving the quality of relationships in The League's building. This is something that you can't simply motivate your staff to do with your passion; you have to build systems and processes to enable this to happen.

Her staff started doing morning circles across the building every day with all of her students, from elementary to high school. This allowed time and space in their school schedule for relationship building. We gave staff prompts to help them create topics to use for the circles, but also taught them the power of having students come up with their own prompts. The teachers started to lower their hierarchical perspective of "I'm the educator, you're the student," and began to see their students expressing emotions, passions, hobbies, and struggles in a safe, consistent structure. The students also got to see their educators as human beings, not just someone they wanted to fight after jumping off the bus.

In the end, this restorative framework led to improving outcomes for Stephanie's students and eliminating the need for any more out-of-school suspensions at one of the toughest schools in

NYC. The magic was in relational and forgiveness science. It was in understanding that every behavior has a reason and that when we take intentional steps and interventions, we can increase the quality of relationships, the quality of the school environment, and create accountability through processes rather than reactive responses.

The Challenge: Consequences Need to Teach Empathy, Repair, and Replacement Skills

When I was a kid, I stayed with my grandfather off and on. He had a house in Marion next to a big hill with an alley behind it. I was about 13 when I began to carry a small pistol with me and walk up and down the alley with my skateboard, checking which car doors were unlocked. If I found one open, I would sometimes steal something from the car and then take off, knowing I could get away by flying down the hill on my skateboard. Sometimes I'd get in trouble with my parents and had to explain why I had something new, but I always gave a quick excuse or said I traded for it. I didn't really understand why I was doing this. The gun made me feel invincible. I was bored and chasing conflict; I'd pick fights and come home with black eyes. No amount of punishments, detention, or even running from the police made me stop.

The last time I broke into a car, it was because I unexpectedly received a lesson in empathy. The day after I had taken something, I saw someone crying as they frantically searched their back seat. I realized then how cruel what I was doing was and stopped completely. This is why, when I was first trained in restorative justice, I immediately recognized the power of these practices. It can be transformative to see the hurt you've caused and then to work with that person to fix it—for their healing and your own. Just as seeing that person crying in their car stopped me in my tracks, I have shown kids how their actions affect others and witnessed how life-changing and corrective those experiences can be in stopping the behavior from continuing. It is significantly more impactful than a short talk or a consequence with no feelings involved, or even a suspension. The formula for doing this is easy, and empathy is contagious.

I understand school discipline, not just because I was someone who became desensitized to punitive discipline growing up but because I have been a school administrator at two high schools with complex and diverse needs. I understand the need for speed and to juggle several situations at the same time— trying to prioritize and triage issues as they arise while still keeping up with all your duties as an educator. Teachers and school administrators need a consistent, systematic, and tiered supportive approach to discipline in the classroom for office-managed behaviors. When we overcomplicate discipline, like requiring staff to ask a set of restorative questions each time before making a decision, I usually see gaps in consistency and follow-through. Overcomplication of multiple paths to "discipline" can cause misunderstandings between teachers, students, and families over what the consequence is. Also lowering expectations can leave students without a clear understanding of how to act without causing harm or disruptions. Sometimes it can even lead them to gamify the discipline system by trying to find loop holes instead of focusing on just learning.

Punitive discipline does teach the lesson that there will be a consequence, but typically that consequence will need to stimulate a fear response to change the behavior; this is typically done in the hopes of scaring kids into not continuing the behavior. But, what happens when the student doesn't understand what to do instead? We just say, "Don't do that again," but what if they don't know how to act when someone kicks their desk? Or what to do when someone calls them a name that makes them feel sad? We have to give a consequence for an inappropriate way they responded to their trigger, but we must use logical consequences to teach.

Because a logical consequence connects to the behavior, kids learn either a new way to handle the trigger next time or realize how their behavior impacted others. This creates pathways to develop empathy.

Schools need to understand that they are a complex ecosystem and each student and adult needs support as a stakeholder. We must map out how they all affect each other and when harm happens, what is the most appropriate, consistent, and teaching way to fix it. We also have to acknowledge that we are a large determinant of how the culture in this complex ecosystem will feel. In a school building with fewer adults, each one is perceived with a higher amount of respect and are seen as a vital source of safety for these kids. Each adult impacts several different students at the same time for hours. So, if you are dysregulated/angry/resentful toward another part of your ecosystem, the entire ecosystem will feel that greatly.

Adults are the model for regulation, accountability, and soft skill development. When we teach through our actions, students pick up on these practices much more quickly. This also is the easiest teaching method, no curriculum needed.

The Strategy: Increasing Accountability with Logical Consequences

Strong data trends clearly show the effectiveness of logical discipline. According to the *Journal of Educational Research*, students who understand the consequences of their actions are less likely to repeat negative behaviors. They develop a stronger sense of accountability and are more engaged in their learning.

Professor Jane Nelsen's studies show that logical consequences not only reduce misbehavior but also enhance students'
social skills and emotional intelligence. Students who experience
logical consequences are:

- Three times more likely to develop self-regulation
- Four times more likely to show empathy toward others
- Five times more likely to engage in positive peer interactions

These statistics clearly show an easy way to also improve
critical executive functioning skills in students through discipline.

Unlike punishments, logical consequences are determined
by the actions of the student. They are fair, respectful, and
designed to teach accountability by helping the student understand how their behavior impacts others.

Meet Demarcus, who always ends up needing a redirection.
Whether it's making noises, throwing paper, or chopping it up
with his friends, Demarcus is constantly creating challenges for
his teacher, Ms. Garcia. She's tried everything from tough talks,
calls home, and referrals to the office, but nothing seems to work

long-term. Until one day, she decides to try a different approach: logical consequences.

One afternoon, Demarcus was dysregulated, throwing crumpled paper during a math lesson. Instead of sending him to the office with a referral, Ms. Garcia mentally took note of the behavior and waited to address it until after the class began doing some partner work. She approached Demarcus with a calm, regulated tone, asking him to come chat with her at her desk for a moment. Once they got to her desk, Demarcus pulled up a chair and she started:

"Demarcus, I noticed you were throwing paper during our lesson. Can you tell me what was going on with that?"

Demarcus shrugged, avoiding eye contact. "I was bored."

Ms. Garcia said, "I get that you think this math lesson might have been boring. But throwing paper disrupted the flow of my teaching. How do you think that affects other students or me?"

Demarcus looked up, sensing her genuine interest with her eye contact/tone/non-verbals, he said, "I guess it might have distracted you or them."

"Exactly," Ms. Garcia said. "So, what do you think would be a fair way to make up for the disruption?"

Demarcus thought for a moment. "Maybe I could help clean up the paper I threw and missed by the trash can?"

Ms. Garcia smiled, "That sounds like a great idea. And how about we also find ways to make math more interesting for you when we chat next?" Demarcus nodded, feeling heard and a newfound sense of responsibility as he received a quick empathy-based discipline lesson with a small logical consequence.

According to a study in the *Journal of Educational Psychology*, students who experience logical consequences are more likely to develop intrinsic motivation and self-discipline. Like Demarcus, they're not just behaving to avoid punishment; they're learning to respect the community and their role within it. Logical consequences should connect directly to the misbehavior, be delivered respectfully, and be fair in their execution. This trifecta ensures that consequences are impactful without being harsh.

How-To Guide: Implementing Logical Consequences

Here's your step-by-step guide to start bringing logical consequences into your classroom.

Step 1: Identify the Reason Behind the Behavior

- **Observe and Understand:** Pay attention to the behavior and consider the underlying reasons. What's the student trying to communicate through their actions?
- **Discuss with the Student:** Have a calm conversation with the student about their behavior. Use open-ended questions to understand their perspective.
  - *Example:* "Demarcus, I noticed you were throwing paper during class. Can you tell me what was going on?"

Step 2: Establish the Connection

- **Explain the Impact:** Help the student see how their behavior affects others.
  - *Example:* "Throwing paper distracts your classmates and makes it hard for them to focus."
- **Foster Empathy:** Encourage the student to put themselves in others' shoes.
  - *Example:* "How would you feel if someone was distracting you while you were trying to learn?"

Step 3: Brainstorm Logical Consequences

- **Collaborate on Solutions:** Involve the student in coming up with a fair consequence that directly relates to their behavior.
  - *Example:* "What do you think would be a good way to make up for the disruption?"
- **Ensure Relevance:** The consequence should be directly related to the misbehavior.
  - *Example:* "Since the classroom got messy, would you be willing to help clean it up after school?"

Step 4: Implement and Follow-Up

- **Agree on the Plan:** Ensure both you and the student are clear on the consequence and its purpose.
  - *Example:* "Great, so you'll help clean up after school today. Does that sound fair?"
- **Reflect and Review:** After the consequence has been carried out, discuss how it went and what the student learned.
  - *Example:* "How did it feel to help clean up? What did you learn from this experience?"

Quick Tips: Psychological Safe Classroom Environments

Safe expectations are the building blocks beneath empathy and learning. They also make logical consequences possible. Within a psychologically safe environment, students understand that consequences are not punishments but opportunities to repair and grow, rather than intended to cause shame or fear.

(continued)

The skill of understanding empathy grows where people feel secure enough to risk being seen and seeing other people. Psychologists and organizational experts, like Amy Edmondson, define psychological safety as a climate where individuals believe they can speak up, make mistakes, and learn, without fear of punishment or humiliation. In classrooms lacking that safety, students, and even adults, are far less likely to share, take perspective, or ask vulnerable questions (Hough, 2022).

In educational research, evidence continues to grow that teacher empathy is linked to lower stress and higher engagement. For example, one recent cross-contextual study found that students perceiving greater teacher empathy reported reduced anxiety and depression, mediated by deeper classroom engagement. There is also another report that argues that empathy-based relational climates encourage students to enter dialogue and reveals imperfect thinking (Ampofo et al., 2025). It's important for students to think critically that they must be able to unpack their thoughts through constructive conversations.

How to build safety into expectations

Strategy	What it looks & sounds like in class	Why it deepens empathy
Co-construct agreements	On day 1 (or start of a new unit), ask: "What helps you feel respected, heard, and challenged?" Use student input to co-create norms for the classroom.	Students then own the space. When they help build the "rules of safety," they feel connected to the purpose of the expectations.
Explain the why	Don't just say "No phones." Instead: "Phones are a distraction to what's going on around us. Especially in class, a place where we are learning together."	Knowing the purpose of the expectation invites relational insight into the expectation, not just compliance.

Be consistent and transparent	Use the same language in reminders, feedback, and responses. If you deviate from the plan, explain why.	Consistency reduces ambiguity. Transparency keeps trust alive.
Check in on the classroom climate	Use brief anonymous or low-stakes surveys in mid-unit: "Do you feel safe to share ideas? Why or why not?" Then you can adjust strategies mid-unit that might not be creating the safe environment we want.	You're signaling that safety is through open dialogue and sharing feedback and not just complying and listening to others.

Top 10 Negative Classroom Behaviors and Logical Consequences

Disruptive Talking

Behavior: Constant talking during lessons.

Logical Consequence: Assign the student to help lead a discussion or presentation, emphasizing the importance of listening and speaking at appropriate times.

Additional Options:

1. Create a "silent signal" for you to use with the student when they are being slightly disruptive to not make them feel opposition, which sometimes comes out with a verbal redirection if student is sensitive.

2. Designate a specific time during the day for the student to share their thoughts or ask questions. This ensures the student feels heard while maintaining the flow of the lesson.

3. Pair the student with a "talking buddy" for focused discussions during appropriate times, such as group work or break periods. This allows the student to express themselves in a controlled manner.

Inattentiveness

Behavior: Not paying attention or daydreaming during class.
Logical Consequence: Have the student summarize the lesson or key points for the class, helping them stay engaged and accountable.
Additional Options:

1. Implement regular check-ins by asking the student specific questions about the lesson throughout the class. This keeps them alert and involved in the ongoing discussion.

2. Assign a peer mentor who can help the inattentive student stay focused by encouraging them to participate through positive modeling.

3. Use interactive activities, such as quick quizzes, hands-on projects, or group discussions, to keep the students' attention and make learning more engaging.

Incomplete Homework

Behavior: Consistently not completing homework.
Logical Consequence: Provide a designated time during recess or after school for the student to complete their homework, reinforcing responsibility.
Additional Options:

1. Set up a homework contract with the student that outlines clear expectations and consequences. Both the teacher and student sign the contract to formalize the agreement.

2. Offer a homework club that meets regularly to provide additional support and a quiet space for completing assignments. This can also foster a sense of community among students.

Defiance

Behavior: Refusal to follow instructions.

Logical Consequence: Assign the student a leadership role in a class activity to channel their defiance into positive leadership.

Additional Options:

1. Hold a private meeting with the student to discuss their feelings and reasons for defiance. This one-on-one time can help uncover underlying issues and build a better teacher–student relationship.

2. Use a behavior reflection sheet that the student fills out to reflect on their actions and how they could have handled the situation differently. Review the sheet together.

3. Develop a personal goal-setting plan with the student, outlining specific behavior goals and the steps needed to achieve them. Regularly review and adjust the plan as needed.

Bullying

Behavior: Teasing or bullying classmates.

Logical Consequence: Facilitate a restorative justice meeting where the student must listen to how their actions affected others and work on a plan to make amends.

Additional Options:

1. Involve the student in a community service project that requires them to work with others and develop empathy. This can help them understand the impact of their actions on others.

2. Assign a book or video and have them unpack a part of it through the lens of empathy and have the student complete

a related project or discussion. This can help the student develop a deeper understanding of empathy and perspective taking.

3. Pair the student with a mentor, such as an older student or staff member, who can provide guidance and support. Regular check-ins with the mentor can help monitor progress and address issues.

Tardiness

Behavior: Frequently arriving late to class.
Logical Consequence: Have the student make up missed time during lunch or after school, emphasizing the importance of punctuality.
Additional Options:

1. Implement a tardiness tracker where the student records their arrival times. Reward improvements with positive reinforcement, such as praise or small incentives.

2. Set up an alarm system with the student, either through a physical alarm clock or a phone reminder, to help them manage their time better and arrive on time.

3. Discuss any underlying issues with the student that may be causing their tardiness, such as difficulties at home or transportation issues. Work together to find solutions.

Destructive Behavior

Behavior: Damaging school property.
Logical Consequence: Require the student to help repair or clean up the damaged area, teaching respect for property and responsibility.

Additional Options:

1. Create a class project to restore the damaged area together. This promotes a sense of community and collective responsibility among students.

2. Assign the student a responsibility that promotes care for the environment, such as taking care of classroom plants or organizing recycling efforts. This helps them develop respect for their surroundings.

3. Hold a discussion with the class about the impact of destructive behavior on everyone. This can include stories or examples of how such actions affect the school community.

Cheating

Behavior: Copying work or cheating on tests.

Logical Consequence: Have the student redo the assignment or test honestly and discuss the importance of integrity and effort.

Additional Options:

1. Have the student do additional homework or a test as a consequence. This could show them that, if you are dishonest and try to get out of something, you can have double the work next time.

2. Provide additional study support or resources to help the student feel more confident in their abilities and reduce the temptation to cheat. This could include tutoring sessions or study groups.

3. Set up an accountability partner for the student, who can help them stay on track with their studies and encourage honest behavior. This peer support can be highly effective.

Exclusion

Behavior: Excluding peers from group activities.

Logical Consequence: Assign the student to a group activity where they must work cooperatively and include others, fostering teamwork and inclusivity.

Additional Options:

1. Implement a buddy system that pairs the student with different classmates for various activities, encouraging inclusivity and diverse interactions.

2. Discuss the impact of exclusion with the class, using stories or role-playing activities to illustrate how it feels to be left out and the importance of including everyone.

3. Plan team-building exercises that require all students to work together to achieve a common goal. This helps build stronger relationships and a sense of belonging among students.

Lack of Effort

Behavior: Not putting effort into assignments or activities.

Logical Consequence: Have the student redo the work with a focus on quality, perhaps providing extra support or a peer mentor to help them improve.

Additional Options:

1. Set clear, achievable goals with rewards for the student. Break larger tasks into smaller, manageable steps and celebrate milestones to keep them motivated.

2. Offer additional help or tutoring sessions to provide the student with the support they need to succeed. This can be done during lunch, after school, or through online resources.

3. Create an option for them to do an extra-credit assignment about something they find passionate to help engage them and to break the ice of the uncomfortability of redoing the assignment.

Logical Consequences: Top Four Referral Behaviors for School Administrators

Now for the most challenging behaviors that school administrators frequently encounter with logical consequences. Here are the top four behaviors that often result in referrals, along with clear, actionable consequences to effectively manage and mitigate these issues.

Chronic Absenteeism

Behavior: Frequently missing school without valid reasons.
Logical Consequence: Schedule a meeting with the student and their parents to discuss the importance of regular attendance and create an attendance improvement plan.
Additional Options:

1. Assign the student a school-based mentor who can provide daily check-ins and support to encourage attendance.
2. Implement an attendance tracking system with rewards for improved attendance, such as certificates or special privileges.
3. Collaborate with community resources to address underlying issues that may be contributing to absenteeism, such as transportation difficulties or family challenges.

Severe Disrespect

Behavior: Showing severe disrespect to staff or students, including verbal abuse.

Logical Consequence: Require the student to participate in a restorative justice session, where they must listen to the affected individuals and make a plan to repair the harm caused.

Additional Options:

1. Teach them empathy through an activity that unpacks how people feel when you do certain behaviors. This could be through a shared story with questions or having them perspective take through reflecting and writing out the situation with different points of view.

2. Implement a behavior contract that includes specific expectations and consequences for disrespectful behavior, signed by the student, parents, and administrators.

3. If behavior continues, organize a series of meetings with the student, parents, and a school counselor to address underlying issues and develop a comprehensive behavior improvement plan.

Fighting/Physical Aggression

Behavior: Engaging in physical fights or aggressive behavior.

Logical Consequence: Suspend the student for a short period and require them to attend a reentry meeting with parents and administrators to discuss behavior expectations and consequences.

Additional Options:

1. Enroll the student in a conflict resolution or anger management program to help them learn non-violent ways to handle disputes. They should also understand their triggers, cues, and coping skills when they notice either one of these happening.

2. Arrange for the student to perform community service within the school, such as assisting with maintenance or helping in the cafeteria, to foster a sense of responsibility in the space where they were aggressive or fought in.

3. Provide ongoing counseling or therapy to address underlying issues contributing to aggressive behavior and support the student's emotional well-being.

Substance Abuse

Behavior: Using or possessing drugs or alcohol on school property. **Logical Consequence:** Suspend the student and require them to complete a substance abuse counseling program before returning to school.
Additional Options:

1. Collaborate with local substance abuse prevention programs to provide educational workshops and resources for the student and their family.

2. Implement random drug testing as a condition for continued attendance, with clear guidelines and support for positive results.

3. Create a peer support group for students struggling with substance abuse, providing a safe space for discussion and mutual encouragement.

What Could Go Wrong: How to Stay Consistent and Where's the Time?

Consistency builds trust. Remind kids of the expectations and implement consequences fairly and consistently as a disciplinarian. There is so much teaching that goes into every discipline conversation or redirection on both sides. If students perceive that you're reliable and predictable, they'll be more likely to respect the boundaries you set without feeling a need to be oppositional. This is normally caused by kids feeling not respected, unfairly treated, emotionally or physically unsafe in their environment, struggling with mental health challenges, or experiencing a lack of consistency with the adults in their lives. Consistency also helps you avoid the appearance of favoritism, which can quickly break trust in communities.

Being consistent doesn't mean being inflexible. It means applying expectations and rules in a fair and predictable manner while still considering individual circumstances, needs, and causes of the behavior. When students know to expect consequences that are fair—consequences that match their behavior and are progressive—they feel more secure.

Consistency is also about involving students in the process of building expectations in the community, so they feel a sense of ownership and responsibility.

Imagine a classroom where the expectations are clear and everyone knows what's expected of them. There's no confusion or ambiguity. Students understand the consequences of their actions and feel a sense of fairness in how rules are applied since they helped co-create them. This consistency builds trust and respect, creating a positive learning environment.

Dealing with Resistance

You might also have students who will resist participating in these conversations. This is normal. You are asking someone to be vulnerable with you, which might never have been modeled for them. Give students space to express themselves and be themselves, which means sometimes just listening and asking the class questions that help them consider the people around them.

Ask questions like, "What causes harm to others in our community?" and "How do we repair harm when it happens in our community?" This helps create a shared understanding around what "our community" is and how they all impact each other. Communities (micro-communities is the classroom to macro-communities which is the full school) then actively build trust through providing spaces where when harm is caused, we repair it and fix it with the parts of the community that were impacted.

Also, resistance is natural, especially when students are accustomed to traditional discipline methods. I always tell educators, "Be calm-assertive" when redirecting resistance. Don't jump into a power struggle or a debate; simply ask the resistant person to pick one of two options and give them time and space to make their decision without sounding condescending or making them feel blame, shame, or embarrassment. I also typically don't tell a student what the consequence will be in advance. If I tell an already resistant student exactly what the consequence will be, the student might treat it like a calculation: "Is the behavior worth the consequence?" If they decide the consequence isn't too bad, they might keep misbehaving.

Violent and Threatening Behavior

While I believe it's essential for students and adults to approach others with empathy, it is equally important to have strong boundaries. When strict boundaries are broken, I believe the first offense should be taken seriously with concrete, logical consequences and that we must act firmly and swiftly when a student's behavior threatens the safety of others or themselves.

This is for behaviors such as threats of violence or harm communicated in any form, any committed assault, patterns of disturbing or violent comments, weapons, drugs, and sexual maladaptive behaviors.

I have worked in some of the most complex schools all around the world, including schools often labeled the most violent or dangerous. I have seen schools go too easy on a major harm causing first-time negative behavior, which can lead to lasting harm. It leaves educators burned out and fearful, students overwhelmed or scared, and families anxious and less willing to engage. It's important for us to understand the impacts, level of harm, and make decisions best for the safety of our school community.

I have also worked to support healing after these events and conducted in-depth interviews with families, students, and educators before facilitating conflict resolution practices with all the affected individuals. When we leave a part unresolved, it starts to erode trust in the system. This is why it is so important to identify everyone who was impacted and how they were affected after harm is done. To repair this level of harm, everyone affected needs a voice at the table to help shape the plan to repair and to express what they need to feel whole again. This plan then needs to be reinforced by skill development of the person that acted out and a plan to continue to develop and assess the skills.

It is also important to review your school's threat assessment best practices when these types of behaviors occur. Strict consequences should be given to address every layer of harm, and clear safety measures should be in place to ensure the behavior doesn't happen again before reintegrating the student that displayed these behaviors. If it does continue, a clear and previewed consequence must be understood by all parties.

Manipulative Behavior

It's important to be mindful that students can manipulate forgiveness/restorative practices and it's important to match words with actions. We understand that some kids and adults can pretend they are sorry for a situation and say it meaningfully but not mean it. This is often seen in oppositional defiant disorder or even psychopathic types of behaviors. If I notice this in someone else, I typically adjust the way I communicate with this person moving forward until they build trust back with me or show me "proof" they have done what they said they would.

As a youth worker, I worked with several kids who pretended to show sympathy and empathy after committing violent offenses. I encountered only a small number of youth like this, and I was working with the most complex populations of youth. Even when I would work on the residential unit with a youth displaying psychopathic traits in a conduct disorder diagnoses, I would quickly realize that my entire relationship with this person had to be very logical, with well defined boundaries that allowed for no wiggle room for breaking rules. I also realized I had to shut down conversations quickly when they would display maladaptive or manipulative communication.

Using these strategies, I got along with these youth well and operated under mutual respect with a clear relationship. I grew up with someone who had psychopathic traits and knew how to avoid conflict and how to communicate with someone with these traits. They sometimes seek validation by making you have an emotional response to something they say or do. It's important to show little emotions and affect, using calm, assertive redirections when this occurs.

Parent Huddle

Now, let's bring logical consequences into the home. Parents play the most crucial role in reinforcing positive behavior and creating an empathetic human. Here's how parents can apply these practices at home:

1. Communicate Openly

Encourage open communication with your child. Regularly check in and give them an opportunity to share their thoughts, feelings, and experiences. Be supportive and non-judgmental. Ask open-ended questions like "How was your day?" and "Is there anything you want to talk about?" These open conversations show your child that you care and are interested in their life.

2. Set Clear Expectations

Establish clear and consistent expectations/rules at home. Involve your child in setting these expectations to increase their investment. Explain the reasons behind the expectations and the consequences of breaking them. This helps your child understand the importance of following guidelines and provides a sense of structure and security.

3. Model Behavior

Modeling positive behavior is one of the most effective ways to teach children. Demonstrate respectful and empathetic behavior in your interactions. Children learn by observing how you handle conflicts and challenges. Show them how to communicate calmly, especially when you're upset, listen actively, and resolve issues together and constructively. Your behavior sets the tone for how they will respond to similar situations.

4. Use Logical Consequences

When a child makes a mistake, focus on accountability and learning rather than punishment. For example, if they break a sibling's toy, a logical consequence could be helping to repair or replace it.

Steps to follow:

1. Name the issue: "When you broke your brother's toy, it upset him."
2. Explore the impact: "How do you think he felt?"
3. Collaborate on a solution: "What can you do to make this right?"

This approach teaches kids to take responsibility while fostering empathy and problem-solving and decision-making skills. Encourage them to think critically and come up with constructive solutions with you. This approach isn't just about managing behavior; it's about modeling life skills, teaching accountability, and having less conflict in the future.

You can go over a couple common scenarios your family runs into together and help them understand the expectations for each person to make sure the behavior doesn't continue and, if it does, what is the consequence implemented.

5. Follow-Up and Support

Monitor your child's progress and provide consistent support. Celebrate their successes and guide them through challenges. Regular check-ins and positive reinforcement help reinforce good behavior and build trust. Consistent follow-up and support are essential for reinforcing positive behavior.

Bringing restorative practices into the home creates a consistent and supportive environment for your child. It reinforces the lessons they're learning at school and helps them develop important life skills. Remember, this is a journey. Implementing restorative practices takes time, patience, and commitment. But the rewards are worth it. By unveiling the science of discipline, we can create classrooms and homes where respect, accountability, and empathy thrive. Keep pushing forward, stay motivated, and remember—you've got this.

4

Leading with Empathy
A Blueprint for Emotional Intelligence

"Empathy is the experience of foreign consciousness in general, irrespective of the kind of experience through which it is grasped."
—Edith Stein

Seek to Understand: She Woke Up to a New Reality That No One Understood

One fall break, I loaded my son Asher and a few of his longtime friends into a van for a road trip to see the ocean for the first time. The two-day drive gave us time to talk and share stories. Among them was Bria, a 16-year-old with a sensitive but outgoing personality. In all the years I've known Bria, I noticed she liked to push against authority a little, but nothing that was largely oppositional. She had a big, supportive, and deeply connected family.

Quick to speak her mind, she was rarely dishonest. That's why, when she chose to share her story with us in the car, it was easy for me to accept her story as truth.

Months earlier, Bria had collapsed at school and fallen into a short-term coma from a drug overdose. All she could remember in the time leading up to this was asking the teacher if she could get a drink of water and stopping in the bathroom. Soon after leaving the bathroom, she returned to the water fountain, and as she walked back to class, she noticed something strange. "I remember walking past people, and their faces started to melt, and then they were like demon faces and laughing at me," she said nervously to the car.

Bria shared that by the time she returned to the classroom, her pupils were huge. Grabbing her phone, she showed us a picture of her eyes fully dilated and her face bright red, her peers laughing in the background. This was the last thing she remembered before passing out in class. She woke up nearly 24 hours later in the hospital, with her father by her side. She underwent a full drug screen and tested positive for two substances, but not marijuana, which, in my experience, is unusual, since this is often the first substance used at her age before harder drugs.

She said, "I promise, I didn't take any drugs before and don't remember taking anything. If I did take something, I would feel really bad, but I must have just blacked it out. I'm really sorry, but I don't know what happened." She later learned from the principal, after watching the surveillance video, that there had been one other person in the bathroom when she entered. Whether she was spiked or not, she still doesn't know.

This, unfortunately, is where the story gets worse and when the harassment, bullying, and labeling by teachers and students started happening.

One peer, who she turned down earlier in the year when he asked for a date, said to her one day, "I wish you had just died," randomly as she was walking between classes.

Less than a month after the incident, Bria asked her teacher a question in class, and her peers laughed. The teacher mockingly asked, "Are you high again?" Bria felt like the teachers now looked at her suspiciously, and her peers were quick to call her names, "All the teachers think I'm just this druggy, and even kids call me 'The girl that OD'd.'" A few girls in her neighborhood even started picking fights, and parents began to say passive-aggressive comments to her.

After the incident, I noticed Bria's temperament began to change, where she would quickly break out into tears with emotional outbursts of anger toward her siblings. During our fall road trip, I took the kids up in a hot air balloon. It was everyone's first time, but Bria in particular immediately froze and couldn't speak or move for about five minutes. She later doesn't remember freezing.

In the years I've known Bria and from what her siblings have shared, these behaviors were not typical for her until after the incident occurred. The bullying may have caused more harm than the actual overdose. It's hard to know why her emotions shifted so much, but the situation was traumatizing, and the way her world changed once she woke up from the coma was something she was not at all ready for.

Empathy is a conscious act of perception. It takes intentional awareness and effort to see and feel what someone else is experiencing. I begin this chapter with this story because Bria wishes more teachers had led with empathy in her situation. She believes that she was drugged by using the same drinking fountain that was linked to another similar situation. Whether Bria was spiked or made a one-time mistake that she can't remember and that almost cost her life, she did not deserve to be bullied by her peers, teachers, and families during such a difficult experience. It broke my heart that she went through this and is still going through it today. Bria and her family gave me permission to share her experience (though names have been changed out of respect) to help show other educators that sometimes we know only a bit of a story and need to be curious.

Like Bria's peers, kids are looking to educators and the adults in the room to set the tone and model how to treat others. Because of this, we need to make conscious efforts to understand other people's stories without bias toward what we think might have happened. We must seek truth and think about what they might be feeling. Then we must act in our highest ability to understand with empathy and support the people around us, especially when we know they are going through something rough.

The Challenge: We Often Try to Teach Empathy Without Practicing It

The best way for kids to learn emotional intelligence is by seeing adults consistently model and explain healthy ways of expressing a range of emotions.

One of the essential elements of emotional intelligence is empathy—the ability to recognize, understand, and share what someone else is feeling. If you grew up with an adult in your life who regularly tried to understand your feelings, apologize to you, and express their own emotions with explanations, you have a high likelihood of feeling empathy easily. If you grew up without those things, you have a higher likelihood of having to be more intentional about feeling empathy when communicating with others.

Empathy is an exploratory emotion where we examine and feel something through a vulnerable perspective, which is sometimes outside of our own safe perspective. It is not an easy thing to teach, and that's why modeling it constantly in how we communicate is important. Modeling empathy is how we help our students to develop it, but we can't expect them to learn this skill if we don't practice it ourselves.

One great thing about empathy is that it leads to quick bursts of happiness. A study from the University of North Carolina at Chapel Hill in 2014 found that people who expressed and actively thought about how they are experiencing empathy three to four times a day had significant and measurable improvements not only in their daily happiness but in satisfaction in life overall (Source: Fredrickson, B. L., et al. "Affect and health behavior." American Psychologist, 2014).

Our environment also is a challenge. The less we are surrounded by empathy, the less likely we are to practice it ourselves. And without experiencing empathy as we are developing our thoughts about a situation, we begin interpreting those situations through our own feelings instead of considering what others might be experiencing.

When people around us feel misunderstood, dismissed, or unsafe, it creates a space of distrust within the relationship that can only be repaired by mutual acknowledgment and actions toward fixing the harm. This is really tough to do if you don't recognize the harm you've caused or identify it by understanding others through an empathetic lens. You can see how this cycle could go round and round, right?

I believe empathy is the answer to helping people feel connected to the world around them.

The Strategy: Leading with Empathy

We have countless technologies to easily connect us to each other, yet most people feel more isolated and lonelier than ever before. I wonder if maybe we aren't feeling lonely but rather experiencing a lack of collective empathy. I believe that not feeling empathy within our interactions triggers intense feelings of loneliness. While we can't control how others treat us or respond, we can lead by example by connecting with people around us who can strengthen our own capacity for empathy by practicing relational safety through understanding other's feelings.

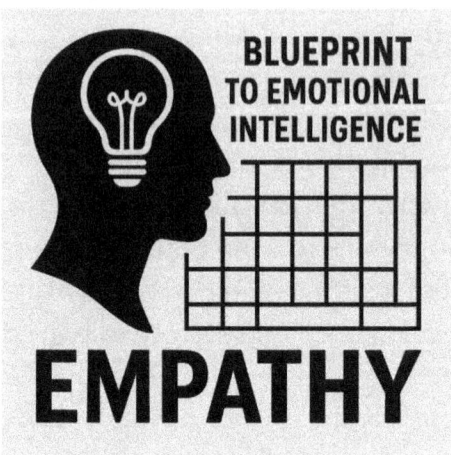

The blueprint to emotional intelligence includes two focuses: quality of the process and quality of the space you create around you.

In the quality of the process you must develop:

- **Skills** to safely express your range of emotions
- **Competence** to recognize and understand personal emotions and values. Competence to regulate emotions and impulses under pressure
- **Confidence** in your ability to hear people for what they experienced and not just how it makes you feel
- **Knowledge** of what your triggers are and the ability to regulate in order to avoid impulsive behaviors

In the quality of the space you must focus on having:

- **Empathy** as your primary goal in communicating
- **Co-constructing expectations** to set expectations and makes people around you feel safe
- **Values** that shape the way you interact with others and guide you during times when you are dysregulated
- Being **present** and mindful of your verbal and nonverbal communication so others feel safe and confident expressing themselves

When empathy guides the way you communicate, it brings your class together and creates a sense of belonging. It strengthens relationships, builds self-awareness, and improves communication and cooperation. Empathy is also the doorway to compassion, which is key to a classroom where students take accountability and ownership of their actions. While empathy is being able to put ourselves in another's shoes, compassion is putting that feeling into action and responding to another's pain or suffering. Together, they are what drive us to repair harm done—to apologize, make actionable amends, and change the behavior.

Research also shows that empathetic practices directly support adult well-being and shape healthier school climates. When educators and leaders practice empathy with each other and with students, the ripple effects are immediate: staff feels more supported, classrooms become more inclusive, and students learn to model the same skills. A culture rooted in belonging is not only good for student growth; it is also essential for sustaining the adults who guide them every day.

How to Guide: Practicing and Modeling Empathy

Journaling has always been personally helpful to me for goal setting and tracking skill-building. To strengthen your emotional intelligence, you can start by setting a goal for how many times per week you want to try to increase one of the following strategies and track how it makes you feel.

Micro-Moments of Empathy Practice

What It Is   Instead of saving empathy perspective-taking for big conversations, practice quick, small moments of empathy with students throughout the day. It might be just noticing their body language or saying "how's your morning going?" or taking time to really notice how someone around us is feeling.

Why It Works   These small moments help you build the muscle for when discipline situations happen that could trigger rapid dysregulation, taking away our ability to feel empathy. The more we practice tuning into someone else's feelings during neutral or low-stress times, the easier it is for us to understand someone's feelings when we have been hurt by this person. Research on emotional understanding and empathy training shows these micro-practices help our brains build faster and more regulated responses to triggers.

How to Do It   Pick three times during your day when you will pause to notice how a student might be feeling at that moment in class. This strategy has personally helped me better understand how to communicate with the person if you need to step in and help.

Empathy Mapping

What It Is   Before jumping into a conversation after an incident with little understanding, take a moment to do an "empathy map," jotting down what you think the student might be thinking, feeling, needing, and doing right now. Not to judge or fix their problem with a solution, this is just to shift your perspective into a curious state to think about all the potential "what if" scenarios.

Why It Works   When we start by being curious about understanding the other person before engaging, it reduces bias and reactive responses. Once we are ready to engage in a conversation, empathy also helps regulate the other person's nervous system, with them feeling heard and validated. Studies have shown that compassion like this builds our ability to feel calm more quickly. This has been shown to reduce neural threat activation, enabling us to have a stronger ability to self-soothe and regulate our emotions (Source: https://www.nature.com/articles/s41598-020-63846-3?utm_source).

How to Do It   Keep a sticky note nearby or use a blank part of your behavior form. Quickly write four things: what is this student *thinking, feeling, needing,* and *doing*? Then go into the conversation with that lens to help keep you grounded but curious about the assumptions you might be thinking about those areas.

THINKING

What might the student be thinking right now and why?
(Try and interpret the internal story, beliefs, or worries)

_____
_____
_____
_____

FEELING

What emotions is the student showing or signaling?
(Body language, tone of voice, facial cues, and energy level)

_____
_____
_____
_____

NEEDING

What does the student likely need at this moment?
(Examples: clarity, connection, a break, reassurance, structure)

_____
_____
_____
_____

DOING

What behavior is the student showing?
(Describe only what you can observe with no judgments)

_____
_____
_____
_____

TEACHER RESPONSE: *What empathy aligned action will I take next?*

Empathy Rounds

What It Is   Once a week or every other week, get together with one to two other educators and do a quick "empathy round." Each person shares a challenging student moment, and the others reflect back what the student might have been experiencing or needing. The goal is not to problem-solve but to practice empathy and offer a different perspective.

Why It Works   When we intentionally strengthen our empathy lens through social learning, we create more space for authentic connections. Modern neuroscience tells us mirror neurons fire when we listen with empathy. In practice, that means we don't just hear someone's story—we feel into it. This kind of deep listening helps us expand our own capacity for compassion, and it also protects us from the exhaustion that often comes from trying to "fix" others. Instead of draining our energy, empathy becomes a renewable source of connection that actually reduces burnout.

How to Do It   Set aside 10–15 minutes during homeroom, circle time, or a meeting. Invite one person to share a challenging moment. The group reflects back from an empathetic perspective: What might that person have been feeling at the time? What needs might have been present? What might they have been trying to communicate? After the group reflects, the original person responds and shares what felt accurate. Keep the space safe, supportive, and open for exploring emotions. Encourage participants to practice expressing themselves both verbally and nonverbally.

This practice can be used for educators in staff meetings or professional learning circles or with students to build empathy and perspective-taking. In either setting, it strengthens communication, builds trust, and helps participants feel seen and understood.

Be Kind and Rewind

What It Is   After any discipline interaction, take one minute to mentally rewind and notice: Where did I feel empathy? Where did I lose it? What cues from the student could I notice more quickly next time?

Why It Works   Metacognition about your empathy practice builds awareness and growth. Even quick reflections like this rewire the brain and increase self-compassion. It helps educators approach the next moment with more readiness. The easiest and most successful framework is the Gibb's Reflective Cycle created by Graham Gibbs in 1988. It breaks down how to do this reflection in six easy steps to guide your thoughts and self-awareness. Let's go through them.

How to Do It   After a stressful situation or disruptive incident in class, build in a "pause and reflect" moment in the car, at your desk, or between classes.

Ask yourself:

1. **The facts:** What are the facts of what happened? Who was involved? When and where did it happen? What did you do? What did others do in this situation?

2. **Feelings:** What were you feeling and thinking during that time? What emotions did you have, and how did they affect your actions?

3. **Self-evaluation:** What went well and what didn't? Rate yourself on how you handled this situation.

4. **Analysis:** Why did things happen the way they did? Think about behavior, communication, and systems here.

5. **Action plan:** What would you do differently next time? What skills or future support do you need to respond better next time? How will you be ready for this situation in the future?

Scenario: A Teacher Does a "Pause and Reflect" After Handling a Disruption   A teacher had a difficult class where a student shouted in the middle of a test and then the entire class became off track. The teacher responded too quickly and wasn't regulated, so the tone of "I need to talk to you right now at my desk," came off aggressive, and the entire class became silent. The teacher addressed the issue with the student who shouted and later, while the class continues their test quietly, pauses, and reflects on their behavior:

- **The facts:** The student yelled randomly and class became disrupted. I became dysregulated and angry.

- **Feelings:** I was frustrated and confused about why the outburst happened.

- **Self-evaluation:** I handled it well with a redirection for the class, but I was not calm so the redirection came off aggressive with me shouting.

- **Analysis:** The student was doing this as an attention-seeking behavior. I should have quickly regulated myself before redirecting in front of the class.

- **Action plan:** The student will sit in the front row of the class for the next week to help him receive the attention he could have been craving. I owned my behavior with the student and agreed to work on regulating before redirecting.

Normalize Vulnerability

What It Is   When processing with a student after a tense situation or a success, intentionally share your own feelings, struggles, or learning moment with the student. This shows them that vulnerability is safe and that it's normal to hear other people's feelings about why they did what they did. When you model this openness, it helps them feel safe to do the same.

Why It Works   Normalizing vulnerability shows that everyone has emotions, challenges, and areas to grow. When students see vulnerability being modeled, their mirror neurons activate, helping them feel more open to understanding others. Creating a social connection with someone else also releases oxytocin, the happy chemical in the brain, which then promotes trust in that connection.

How to Do It   Build a routine to practice vulnerability and to process feelings with the group. Ask students to share about something they've been struggling with or are proud of but also be the first to model openness with the questions you offer. My favorite way to do this is in a restorative circle. You can ask prompts like these:

- What is something you've recently overcome in your life?
- What am I the most proud of this week and why?
- How do you make people around you feel when they see you?

Quick Tips: Teaching Your Students to Practice Empathy

- **Use "I Feel" Statements**
  Model and practice using "I feel ___ when ___" sentences daily in classrovom discussions.

- **Daily Emotions Check-In**
  Start class with a one-minute check-in: students mark or share how they're feeling using a chart or holding up fingers with their head down.

- **Perspective-Taking Prompts**
  Ask "How do you think they felt?" after reading a story or watching a video.

- **Two-Minute Active Listening Pairs**
  Students take turns speaking for one minute each about a topic with their partner just listening, no interrupting.

- **Restorative Language Scripts**
  Teach sentence frames for repair: "What do you need?"/"What happened?"/"How can we make it right?"

- **Weekly Role-Plays**
  Practice empathy scenarios (e.g., someone being left out, receiving bad news) in short skits.

- **Mirror Neuron Warm-Up**
  Quick body language game: mimic facial expressions and posture to build emotional mimicking and supporting expressiveness in emotions.

- **Journaling for Empathy**
  Five-minute prompts like "Think about a situation that you felt misunderstood. Write down what you wish the

other person would have noticed when you were talking to them?" or "Pick one person in your life right now that you know very well. Write out how they must be feeling and why in as much detail as possible."

- **"Walk in My Shoes" Assignments**
  Assign short writing or reflection tasks, imagining a peer's or character's perspective.

- **Class Agreements on Respect**
  Co-create norms around listening, interrupting, and responding. Then, you can refer back when issues arise.

- **Silent Signals Practice**
  Teach nonverbal cues for support (e.g., thumbs up/down, hand on heart) to promote quiet validation and community participation.

- **Use Think-Alouds for Modeling**
  Say your thoughts out loud in tough moments: "I'm noticing I feel upset, so I'm taking a breath."

Say This Not That: How to Teach Emotional Vocabulary

When we expand students' emotional vocabulary, we give them tools to name what they're experiencing. Naming emotions helps regulate behavior and deepens empathy. The following are some practice scripts for educators that move beyond happy/sad and open space for better conversation.

Practice with:

- "What is a time that you have recently felt **frustrated**? Frustration is typically something getting in the way of what you want to do."

- "What are you the most **hopeful** for in your life right now? Hopeful means you believe something good could happen."

- "Where do you feel **disappointed** the most in school? Disappointed is when we wanted something to go one way, but it went another."
- "What makes you feel the most **proud**? Proud is when you feel good about what you've done or who you are."

Avoid saying:
- "Don't be sad."
- "Stop being mad."
- "You're fine."
- "That's not a big deal."
- "Be happy."

These practice prompts, and phrases to avoid, show students that their emotions are valid and give them precise language to describe what's happening inside. Over time, practicing with five new emotion words each month will expand their capacity to recognize, express, and manage feelings in themselves and others.

What Could Go Wrong

Empathy isn't easy. As much as we want to model understanding and connection, real-world challenges can make it feel impossible to stay empathetic in every moment. If we do, we might even start feeling overwhelmed and emotionally exhausted. I have felt this personally a lot, both from dealing with it directly and from advising school leaders through some of the most difficult situations in their schools. It's important to have time to turn it off and to just enjoy the present moment.

One of the best things about empathy is that it doesn't have to be perfect to be powerful. Even the act of *trying* to understand someone else can teach empathy.

Here are some of the most common things that could go wrong or pushbacks when implementing empathy-driven practices.

"This Takes Too Much Time"

Time is one of the scarcest resources in education. It's easy to worry that slowing down to have restorative conversations or build collective commitments will derail lesson plans or take away from instruction time.

Strategies to Address This Pushback:

1. Start with small moments: Empathy doesn't always require a 10-minute conversation. It can be as simple as pausing to ask, "What's going on today? I've noticed . . . ?"

2. Use peer student help: Train students to help mediate minor conflicts, providing an opportunity to teach conflict resolution skills and freeing up your time for larger issues.

3. Integrate empathy into existing routines: For example, use morning meetings or end-of-day reflections as spaces to practice empathy and resolve conflicts collectively.

"What About Accountability?"

Some people may worry that focusing on understanding emotions will lead to a lack of consequences or lower standards. Actually, empathy and accountability go hand in hand. It helps students understand the impact of their actions and motivates them to make things right.

Strategies to Address This Pushback:

1. Reframe consequences as learning opportunities: Instead of punishment, think about how you can guide students to repair harm.

2. Set clear boundaries: Empathy doesn't mean tolerating harmful behavior. It means addressing it in a way that builds understanding and growth.

3. Celebrate successes: Keep track of moments where empathetic approaches led to accountability and share these examples with stakeholders.

"This Won't Work for Every Student"

It's true; every student is different, and some will resist empathy-driven practices, especially at first. Students with deeply ingrained distrust of adults may be particularly hesitant to engage.

We also know from Dr. Bessel van der Kolk's work that when children experience high levels of trauma or toxic stress, the areas of the brain responsible for empathy, connection, and perspective-taking become underdeveloped (van der Kolk, *The Body Keeps the Score*, 2014). This means many of our most vulnerable students may struggle with empathy, not because they don't care but because their brains have been wired for survival instead of social connection.

Strategies to Address Pushback:

1. **Start with consistency:** Show up every day regulated and with a compassionate approach, even if students might not immediately accept. Over time, this builds trust.

2. **Seek outside support:** Partner with counselors, social workers, or family members to understand and address the deeper needs of complex students.

Parent Huddle: Empathy Opportunities Outside of the Classroom

Empathy practiced at home creates safety in the relationships in the home and safety in the space. It also encourages families to understand each other better, handle conflicts more effectively, discipline and teach through an empathetic lens, and more easily connect to the people around us. We have to understand that, as parents, our children are constantly learning from us by how we interact with them and others around them.

I notice how my son watches me when I communicate with people, from phone calls to looking over my shoulder when I text, and even watching my face in traffic. It's important to realize that we are constantly teaching through our emotional regulation, or lack thereof.

Skill to Practice in Home

Empathetic Listening   The goal of *empathetic listening* is not just to hear the words but to understand and connect with the speaker's feelings and perspective. When kids are upset, frustrated, or just having a big feeling, it's tempting to jump into "fix-it" mode: "You don't need to be mad about that," or "Go to your room until you calm down." But this misses an opportunity for teaching empathy.

Instead of jumping into trying to fix it, try saying the phrase: "It sounds like you're frustrated. Can you explain why you are feeling the way you are?"

It's then important to summarize and reflect on what you hear; this will help validate your child's emotions by knowing they are heard and open the door for deeper conversation.

It's important that if we hear something that triggers us or makes us upset, we don't jump into a fear-based disciplinarian. You're also not agreeing with bad behavior by asking questions before giving a consequence; you're creating space to understand the "why" behind it. This lets your child know that you were truly curious and also helps them unpack how it might have made others feel or impacted others through the questions you ask.

Family Commitments   Remember, one of the principles of emotional intelligence is to focus on *values* that shape how you interact with others and guide you during times of dysregulation. Every family has values, but not every family may name them out loud. Without clear, shared expectations, it's easy for tension and miscommunication to grow. A simple family meeting to write a collective commitment list can be an easy way to bring everyone together and create mutual commitments.

Examples:

- *"We speak kindly to each other, even when we disagree."*
- *"We repair the harm when we hurt someone's feelings."*
- *"We take responsibility for our actions."*

Write them down. Put them somewhere visible. Revisit them when needed (especially after a conflict happens where someone violated the agreements). If you see something getting off track or someone being more dysregulated than usual, schedule a quick family huddle to get everyone aligned on goals or ways to support each other. This is like a timeout at a ballgame to get everyone together and be united.

Repairing Relationships   Apologies shouldn't be forced or empty. Instead of "Say you're sorry!" try coaching your child on how to genuinely make amends:

- Acknowledge the harm (*"I hurt your feelings when I said that"*).
- Express empathy (*"I can see you were sad"*).
- Offer repair (*"I'd like to help fix this. What can I do?"*).

When these conversations happen regularly, they teach children the value of accountability and empathy far beyond meaningless scripts. You can also model repairing relationships. Whenever you lose your temper, it is an opportunity for you to model how to make sincere amends and repair a relationship.

Family dynamics will never be "perfect," but we should strive to create a safe place to learn, develop, and explore the situations with people that care about us. The goal is to keep building strong connections, through simple things like one conversation or successfully time navigating conflict. When parents model these restorative practices at home, they reinforce what we're working to build in schools: an ability to express yourself in an environment through an empathetic lens when communicating.

5

Teaching Self-Regulation

Simple Ways to Teach Regulation and Focus on Our Well-Being

"Feelings come and go like clouds in a windy sky. Conscious breathing is my anchor."

—**Thich Nhat Hanh**

Seek to Understand: Regulation Is Power That Creates True Change

Making decisions regulated, especially after complex and tough situations, is crucial to make sure that you make the *best* decision. Learning regulation isn't always a natural skill for everyone either. So it's important to teach this skill, and I hope this story will show you the power of learning it in a multifaceted way.

I don't think there is any story better in the world that would describe the power of this skill more than the story of my friend, Dee Dee. She took regulated clear action even after immense hardship and now is making substantial positive change in thousands of lives. Dee Dee Taylor has been an advocate for justice since she was four years old, when she first realized she would never get to meet her father outside of prison as he was serving a life sentence he received when he was 19 years old.

After graduating from Jackson College with an associate's degree in criminal justice in 2014 and a bachelor's degree in social work with a minor in psychology from Central Michigan University in 2016, Dee Dee understood deeply that there was reform to be done in the justice system and that the traditional educational instruction was not going to be the launch pad for change across our country.

She then faced another unbearable tragedy of having her sister, Breonna Taylor, wrongfully killed by police. She did not respond with destructive anger or surrender to despair. Instead, she channeled regulated, disciplined grief into intentional action and into policy and structure. Instead of Dee Dee asking for people to riot, she brought people together to take restorative steps and put tools into place to prevent things like this from happening again. "I knew I had to take a healing approach . . . I had to be understanding among both stakeholders, whether it was law enforcement or community." She once said in an interview that she refused to let pain become unregulated rage; instead, she allowed it to become a foundation for true regulated action.

She founded Taylor Made Re-Entry, with a mission to help people coming home from incarceration by providing systems of pre-release and post-release support and programing. She began by focusing her impact where she was, working with her community and in jails and prisons across Grand Rapids, Michigan, all with a laser-focused, healing approach despite what she endured. I personally am honored to be on the board of directors for Taylor Made Re-Entry to fully support the mission of her organization and support Dee Dee, as she is one of the best leaders I've ever met.

The idea is that when someone steps out of prison, society should not leave them adrift and alone to figure things out. She developed a scaffolding support framework from her schooling, knowledge, and lived experiences: case work, mental health, job supports, legal services, and real mentorship.

She didn't stop there at the micro-level (person) but went to the macro-level (systems) and launched Helping Eradicate Adverse Law-Enforcing (HEAL), a national movement to reform police methods, improve accountability, and ensure monitoring of law enforcement practices. Through HEAL, Dee Dee even teaches how to embed regulation into policing culture itself. In her own words: "I'm just a vessel for our community and our people . . . if I don't do it, who's going to do it?" Taylor Made Re-Entry doesn't just dance around in public forums with speeches but works inside prisons, at release, and is deeply integrated into the community.

I respect that she displays clarity around her guiding convictions also: regulations, oversight, and policies. These are the guardrails that prevent harm from metastasizing. Without these things, "good" people become overwhelmed, systems grow rot, and victims become silenced.

Regulation is not the opposite of passion or urgency; regulation is necessary grounding for sustainable passion with urgency. Dee Dee's story is clear proof. She is a steady force in a world that often rewards volatility. Regulation is also an essential life skill that we all need to manage everything from everyday bumps to our hardest challenges.

The Challenge: Managing Our Stress While Teaching Students to Manage Theirs

One evening, I made a mistake with my son. We didn't stick to our schedule, and when it came to our chores, he was dragging his feet. I then pushed him pretty hard, like a coach, to try to get them done before he went back to his mom's house. We had to move some old furniture from our garage. While I was pushing him to move more quickly I said a rude comment about his shoes, he told me a few minutes later that what I just said was mean. I thought about it and apologized to him and corrected what I was trying to say without a tone. He said, "It's okay." We left things on a good note, and after we finished moving the furniture, we went back inside and played a round of *Fortnite* together before his mom picked him up.

I think the challenge is that even though we might be able to teach regulation, how do we model it and/or share vulnerability after we make a mistake, like mine? I know for myself, I sometimes constantly replay an interaction in my head that didn't feel right. My son speaking up and saying "That felt mean" was a brave comment to make, and I felt like I responded to it well. I just felt bad that I hurt his feelings in the first place, but I was proud he communicated this to me. When I hear feedback, I try hard to be regulated, and when my son Asher is regulated while processing a situation, we both hear each other better.

At Purdue University I studied behavioral neuroscience and have always been interested in the brain and the way it responds to situations. The part of the brain I think we are trying to train when it comes to regulating ourselves is the prefrontal cortex. A well-trained prefrontal cortex lets us notice the feeling, create space, and respond thoughtfully instead of reacting impulsively. We also have to understand that to train the brain, we must care for and nurture the nervous system that supports it. When we are triggered in the classroom, our training kicks in or sometimes it doesn't.

Nurturing our nervous systems is ensuring that our emotional and relational networks are soothed sufficiently for our brain's higher-order areas to engage. Emotions should be seen as data to explore, not marching orders to follow. We also regulate by connecting with ourselves or others. We feed this system through truly guiding your decisions with curiosity, empathy, and then courage. Because the brain is neuroplastic, which means it changes its structure and function in response to experience, learning, or injury, we must become flexible in our strategies, adapting as situations shift but guided by our principles of curiosity, empathy, and courage. With practice and relational scaffolding with students/children, our regulation "muscles" strengthen, making thoughtful responses more natural than automatic reactivity.

When adults aren't regulated in an interaction, it historically gets worse. Students are constantly interacting with us, and those interactions are some of the best learning experiences for them, which I've heard through thousands of interviews and circles with students. We have so many opportunities to teach them how to be regulated through just us being regulated or after a mistake being regulated to process it with curiosity and seeking understanding through empathy.

I think the challenge starts with making sure adults have regulation skills and are teaching them in an environment where they personally feel safe and facilitate being safe for others. Education is a vulnerable time in a student's life where they are with peers that they are forming their sense of self around. They have adults in their life who understand them and others that don't. When kids' communication skills are still developing and adults make mistakes while being dysregulated, do these kids hold onto it, let it go, or forgive you if you admit you were wrong? If you don't admit being wrong, what skill are we teaching them?

Another challenge is making sure that the adults have consistent processes and procedures around them to support them with students with varying academic and specific behavioral needs. I have seen in our dynamic needs assessments that teachers often feel safest in schools where discipline is set up with progressively tiered, consistent, and logical consequences. If adults don't feel safe and resourced in their space, it's hard for them to be regulated and then hope to teach regulation skills to students in need. We have to also understand that when we start giving out consequences to students, we want to make sure we aren't doing a behavior that we would not want them to be doing. For example, me roasting my son's shoes when he was going slow with the furniture. I was glad he was able to let me know it hurt his feelings so I had the opportunity to reflect with curiosity and respond with empathy but also because this isn't a behavior I'd want him to do himself.

Nancy Tsai, a pediatrician at Harvard, argues that self-regulation should be taught just like math or reading (Tsai, *Harvard Health Publishing*, 2019). Instead of assuming kids *should* know how to calm down, we need to explicitly teach self-regulation strategies. Many kids come into our classrooms without tools to calm themselves, navigate conflict, or bounce back from mistakes. When dysregulation takes over, the brain shifts into a state of survival, in which the prefrontal cortex, the part responsible for focus, memory, and problem-solving, basically goes offline.

The science is clear: regulated students learn better and live healthier lives. Stress-management practices like mindfulness, breathing, and journaling lower cortisol and reduce anxiety and depression (Zoogman et al., 2015). Emotional regulation also strengthens empathy and social skills, reducing conflict and bullying (Eisenberg et al., 2010). Over time, students who build coping strategies recover faster from setbacks and show greater resilience, especially when supported by caring relationships (Masten, 2014).

But the benefits don't stop with students. Teachers also suffer when regulation isn't prioritized in schools. When adults practice emotional regulation, they experience lower stress and burnout, and classrooms become calmer, safer places for learning (Jennings & Greenberg, 2009). Staying regulated helps teachers de-escalate conflict rather than fuel it (Roeser et al., 2013). Perhaps most importantly, students develop trust and deeper engagement when teachers consistently model empathy and self-control (Pianta et al., 2012).

The challenge, then, is urgent and significantly research backed: if we don't explicitly teach and practice regulation skills in schools, students may likely never learn this skill until a situation gives them a consequence. This could be a small mistake they make or a large one. In seven years working in the juvenile justice system, I've seen, over and over again, many students who made their first unregulated mistake in a big way—and it changed their entire lives. Teaching regulation early on and overcoming these challenges is a huge need for society so we can offset a lot of mistakes that happen out of dysregulation.

The Strategy: Teach Self-Regulation and Stress Management

It always fascinates me how quickly I influence people around me when I'm not being self-regulated even slightly with the tone of something I say. Also, when someone overreacts to a situation, while being disregulated, it feels like someone popped a balloon in a silent room. It takes people by surprise and sometimes is shocking. It takes the air out of the room for a minute and then people have to recalibrate. This is our brain responding with the amygdala after a situation happens, which is the fight/flight/freeze response system in the brain. After we feel safe and that system can "go offline," our prefrontal cortex can start to engage in "what/why/how this just happened? Am I safe? Are others safe in this space? What do we need right now? Is the dysregulated person safe or do they need something?"

When we look at emotions as data to explore, we can first start to unpack what happened before this emotion, then identify what we need to be with this emotion or overcome it, and, finally, reflect on what that emotion teaches us. For example, the way we navigate our stress can be looked at as an overwhelming feeling that we need to avoid or "get rid of," when really it's just a signal to listen to. It's your body and brain's automatic check engine light for you. It tells you something is leading to this stress. When you begin to view these emotions as tools to better understand yourself, then you can use these signals to self-evaluate and see what's within your control and what is not. Then, using your emotions as sensors, you can start to move beyond labeling to taking actions aligned with what you would want.

Prolonged unmanaged and misunderstood emotions can cause us to develop types of desensitized perspectives. When that takes place, it slows down the ability for us to deal with new perspectives or situations in a fair way during conflict, adding stress on our brains. We train our brain when we manage our stress through healthy coping skills and process the causes of stress with curiosity—this builds empathetic teaching experiences around us.

The goal of stress management isn't just our own stress management but helping students understand and process their stress too. They have to get to know their triggers, internal and external, their cues, also internal or external, and understand how to use their coping skills. We can best teach stress management when the adults create learning communities that are safe, structured, predictable, and fair, which fosters safe emotional attachments. We can create a culture where students can manage themselves and support each other, rather than relying solely on the teacher to keep order.

The first step is to **normalize emotional literacy.** We have to move away from quick redirections like "Calm down" or "Stop overreacting" and instead help students name what they're feeling. A simple "I can see you're upset—what's going on?" or "It sounds like you're frustrated. Do you want to talk about it?" gives students permission to feel without shame. Research backs up "naming is taming" emotions, and it can reduce their intensity to help the brain shift from reactive to reflective thinking.

When students have a vocabulary for their feelings, they gain a sense of control over them. That's regulation in practice. Once emotions are named, students can develop healthy release strategies so those feelings don't bottle up and explode later. Journaling, movement breaks, creative outlets like drawing or music, and talking with a trusted mentor are all powerful ways to channel energy constructively. The goal isn't to erase negative emotions but to transform them into actions that don't harm relationships or learning. This approach also reduces the likelihood of stress building to the point of disruptive behavior.

Equally important for regulation is to foster connection, not just compliance. Students who feel isolated often act out, not because they want punishment but because they're searching for belonging. Restorative practices replace "What's wrong with you?" with "What happened to you?" shifting the focus from judgment to curiosity. This change in language signals to students that they are part of a relationship that values them, even when they make mistakes. That sense of belonging acts as a stress buffer, making it easier to stay regulated in challenging moments.

Regulation skills get tested the most during conflict. That's where restorative conflict resolution steps in. The process starts with creating a safe space, focusing on the impact of the behavior, and guiding a conversation that allows all voices to be heard. The goal isn't to assign blame, it's to help students see the ripple effect of their actions and to collaborate on solutions. When students contribute to repairing harm, they're practicing self-regulation, empathy, and problem-solving all at once. From there, the focus shifts to repair and growth. Consequences in this framework are specific, actionable, and connected to the behavior: writing an apology to a peer, helping rebuild something they damaged, or leading a group activity to restore trust. Follow-up conversations and checkpoints keep students accountable while celebrating and validating progress, reinforcing the idea that mistakes are opportunities for learning rather than permanent labels.

Underpinning all these strategies are commitments and agreements built with students, not handed to them, causing a lot of empathy teaching through relational science.

Creating these commitments involves open conversations about the kind of classroom students want, reframing their ideas into positive action statements, and posting the final list where it's visible. Regular check-ins keep the agreements relevant, and inviting students to personalize the document with signatures or artwork fosters ownership. When the adults commit to the same shared values, they create a predictable environment where students know the boundaries, the supports, and the pathways back after missteps. That stability is one of the most powerful stress management tools we can give them.

How to Guide: Three Ways to Teach Regulation Through Environment, Co-regulation, and Expectations

For education around regulation, in this how-to guide I blended a combination of the top research-based models with the neuro-sequential model, developed by Dr. Bruce Perry, around scaffolding stress, including Dr. Dan Siegel's model of window of tolerance and Dr. Lori Desautels' classroom-proven regulation strategies. It's important to combine these best practices in consistent strategies that are easy for educators to regularly practice and to create a feedback loop for success. The following practices will weave in all three.

Key 1: Establishing a Safe and Consistent Environment

When defining the "environment" in schools, the conversation usually is a list of buzz-worthy phrases for Twitter. We picture colorful posters tacked up with washi tape, desks arranged in clever formations, and maybe even a fresh coat of paint that screams "We're fun here!" But if that's all we're focusing on, we're missing the real magic and the real challenge.

Because the true environment of a classroom? That's not something you can see. It's something you feel.

It's that first gut reaction when you step through the doorway. Some rooms feel like a warm hug. Others? Like walking into a storm cloud. And no, that vibe isn't brewed by air fresheners or inspirational cat posters. It's shaped by every glance, every tone of voice, every expectation, spoken or unspoken. It's about whether students walk in and think, "I can be myself here" or "I'd better mask myself to conform."

Think of the classroom environment like air. Students might not always have the words to describe it, but they can tell immediately when something is off. A single look from a classmate, a passive-aggressive comment from a teacher, even an expectation that feels more like a trap than guidance—it all goes into this feeling. And when the air is tense, regulation goes out the window. Instead of learning, kids go into dancing around triggers. That's not where growth happens, and this type of classroom management requires a significant amount of energy to maintain.

Let's think of our classrooms as ecosystems, where regulation and respect are the soil and water. When we nurture those roots, kids don't just behave better—they *feel* better. They show up as their true selves. They're ready to face challenges, make mistakes, and try again. And so are we.

First Step: Establish Positive Emotional Contagion and Relational Safety (Calm Adult Models → Calm Student Mirrors)

When students and educators share a common language for emotions, they can build a foundational environment of relational safety and trust. This reduces the likelihood of escalation, as adults actively model regulated behaviors. Dr. Bruce Perry emphasizes the significance of "emotional contagion," describing how adults' regulated states profoundly affect children's ability to remain calm. Dr. Lori Desautels similarly underscores the need for educators to first manage their own emotional state before responding to dysregulated students. Here is how to set the foundation for emotional contagion:

- **Body–brain check-in:** You can begin each class with a brief routine like this to help kids notice how their mind and body are doing. Educators model openly how they feel and how they're coping—demonstrating vulnerability, openness, and emotional authenticity. Here is a quick script:
  - "Thumb to chest: *Body check*—is your chest tight, loose, or just right?" or "Name three signals you are noticing in your body right now (jaw clenched, stomach flutter, etc.)"
  - "Hand to head: *Brain check*—is your brain feeling focused, fuzzy, or fast today?" or share an "I feel ____" statement.
  - Model this outloud for your students: "Body: shoulders tight. Brain: a little fast."
- **Help kids understand emotional contagion:** Teach students the neuroscience behind emotional contagion, using age-appropriate language (e.g., "mirror neurons" can be said as "brain copying feelings").
  - You can explain how: "Emotional contagion" means feelings can spread from person to person—kind of like a yawn or a giggle that makes others yawn or giggle.
  - Then offer a quick demo: Show your class two faces: worried versus relaxed. Ask: "Which one made your body feel tighter? Which one made your body feel softer or looser?" Or you might ask them all to breathe slowly for 4 counts in and four counts out, and then ask, "How did the room feel after we breathed together?"

Second Step: Build Rhythm and Predictability (Structured Routines → Neurological Safety) Dr. Perry's neurosequential model highlights rhythm and predictability as essential for

stabilizing the nervous system. Similarly, Dr. Desautels emphasizes predictable routines as key to reducing stress and creating
an environment of psychological safety. You can practice co-
regulation by modeling calm with regular breathing exercises,
rhythmic activities, or brief mindfulness exercises.

Rhythmic routines reduce neurological stress responses
and help students internalize strategies that become automatic
responses during emotionally intense moments, enabling quick
de-escalation.

You can create a predictable daily schedule with patterned
breaks (movement, breathing, short reflective moments) between
lessons to maintain regulated brain states. Incorporate "micro-
moments" of rhythmic movement (clapping, drumming, tapping
desks) throughout the day to neurologically prime students for
regulation and attention. You can also introduce "rhythm resets,"
where students and teachers collaboratively pause and reconnect
through rhythmic breathing or bilateral stimulation exercises
(crossing midline, tapping).

Here are some ways to introduce regulation practices into
your classroom:

- **Have a visual schedule** that is easy to see, review it every
  class, and stick to it as closely as possible.

- **Post a regulation menu** where you are straightforward and,
  with cognitively appropriate language, say these are options
  when you aren't regulated (three to five options total):
  "60-sec deep breathing," "5 things I see," "30-sec soft humming," or "soft bilateral tapping."

- **Create a regulation spot** (not a "consequence corner") such
  as a chair angled toward a less crowded area of the room, with
  a simple non-noise timer, and a "reset menu" with options of
  regulation activities and fidget resources. When speaking to

students in that regulation spot, take a co-regulatory stance: slow breath, soft eyes, shoulders relaxed, voice low/slow, and things like having your body angled when you approach.

This works due to creating predictability and safety tools when dysregulation comes up in a confining space kids can't leave like a classroom. These environmental expectations create social-engagement systems that make it easier for students to learn how to work in an environment that they may get dys-regulated in.

Final Step: Use Proven Strategies to Teach Regulation

Regulate → Relate → Reason (the quick chat at the desk)

You can use this right after a small unengaged or disruptive moment and can keep it under two minutes.

- **Step 1: Regulate (5–10 seconds):** Do a quick self-evaluation to check your tone, facial expressions, and words choice after noticing a disruptive situation and before redirecting. This will signal if you need to use a quick coping skill yourself before taking action.

- **Step 2: Relate (30–45 seconds):** You can then bring the student to your desk while the rest of the class is working on a project and calmly say, "I understand getting distracted, but when I heard you talking while I was talking about the group instructions, it also distracted me, which made it hard for me to teach. What's going on today?"

- **Step 3: Reason (45–60 seconds):** Then you can discuss their choices, repairs, and next steps, "If you continue to talk next time I'm trying to instruct, it's going to be hard for me to teach. What do you think you could do to remind yourself to not talk while I'm talking, or what type of consequences will we need to have in place to teach this skill because I have to be able to have one person speaking at a time so everyone understands what is going on."

This worked because you were able to redirect away from peers and avoid using blame, shame, or embarrassment communication. You let the student clearly understand how their behavior is impacting others, teaching empathy, and you also relate to them through curiosity by asking them "what's going on today?" You then restore control without a power struggle, by quickly reviewing next steps and previewing a consequence if the behavior continues to happen.

Dose the Day with Micro-Rhythms (Prevention Over Correction)   It's important to teach coping skills in the calm, not only in the chaos. If the first time a kid tries deep breathing is *during* a meltdown, good luck. Have students practice regulation skills daily (breathing, mindfulness, movement breaks) so they're ready *before* they need them. Here are three micro-routines to run every day:

- **Opening (2 minutes):** Class starts with Resonance Breathing (six breaths/min) or Counting Backwards from 5-4-3-2-1 (name five things you see, four you feel, three you hear, two you smell, one you taste).

- **Mid-class rhythm break (1 minute):** In elementary school you could have your entire class stand and do cross-lateral shoulder taps or slow marching in place. Something that is using a bit of a complicated motion helps regulate our brains quickly and resets us to a level where we can more easily engage.

- **Transition reset (30 seconds):** Before tests, transitions, or leaving class use gentle common reminders: "Last five minutes, that means clean up your desks."

Help Students Create a Mini Regulation Plan by Journaling

You can post a simple Window of Tolerance graphic (green = ready, red = hyper, blue = hypo) on the wall of your classroom. Take a moment to explain what each state can feel like in their minds and bodies to help them identify where on the chart they are:

- *(Red) hyperarousal might feel like:* Fast thoughts, hard to sit still, high energy, using a loud voice, heart thumping.

- *(Blue) hypoarousal feels like*: Heavy body, sleepy or blank, slow thoughts, using a quiet voice, hard to start.

- (green) the *"just-right zone" or within your window of tolerance feels like:* You are ready to learn or play, feeling steady, neither too buzzy nor sluggish, clear headed, focused, using calm voices, able to make good decisions.

Let students personalize a two-item plan: "When I'm red, I choose to journal___. When I'm blue, I ask to choose to do a small movement task in the classroom ___."

This then gives you the opportunity to teach a skill like reflective journaling to the entire class. So then the students know that when they identify as red, even at home, they can use this skill to help them process their experiences with curiosity. This also gives students a safe outlet to process emotions before they spill over.

Studies show that journaling can lower stress, increase emotional regulation, and even improve problem-solving skills. The practice works best when students have options: traditional notebook entries, voice memos, quick one-word check-ins, or even comic strip storytelling. Offering multiple pathways respects different processing styles, which in itself is a form of regulation support.

Building journaling into the school day is also a nonpressured way to teach your entire class. Whether as a two-minute morning check-in, a mid-lesson pause, or an end-of-class reflection, you are showing how easy it is and helping make it a habit. Keeping it private encourages honesty, and modeling the practice as a teacher shows students that self-reflection is a skill for life, not just a classroom task, so go ahead and journal at the same time. Us adults can benefit just as much, using journaling to spot behavior patterns, track our own stress triggers, and test small adjustments.

Key 2: Co-regulation with Our Interactions

What It Is Co-regulation helps kids to regulate their own emotions and return to their window of tolerance by modeling calmness. It can also teach students to learn to handle stress, avoid hasty ill-informed decisions, and even train them to avoid instant gratification. It can empower students, by seeing regulation in action and not being afraid to practice the same skill, to take healthy risks and make mistakes that allow them to learn. Sometimes to re-enter their window of tolerance you have to model what that looks like.

Why It Works Brief, frequent practice builds regulation endurance the way reps build a muscle. Over a few weeks, students internalize the timing and feel of "moving themselves," so you spend less time on behaviors caused by dysregulated students and more on learning.

How To Do It   You can practice co-regulation by noticing if you are having a stress response, and whether you are in hyperarousal or hypoarousal, and then choose a regulation response matched to that state. Practicing and then starting to model this strategy in the classroom helps you stay regulated enough to help co-regulate students just by being around you.

Hyperarousal (amped, high energy, fast talk, fidgety, loud):

- Go slower or become quieter.
- Exhale-heavy breath, orient yourself to your space, try humming.
- Reduce stimulation (lights/inputs), do some tasks that grounded you (sorting, wipe boards).

Hypoarousal (flat, withdrawn, low energy, shut down or "checked out"):

- Sit with upright posture, gentle movement, call-and-response rhythm.
- Take a short inhale/longer exhale but keep a slightly fast tempo.
- Have a cool sip of water, do a brief cold-to-skin reset, or do standing work.

Start with Your Own State

Dr. Desautels teaches that students can't borrow calm from us if we don't have it ourselves. Co-regulation begins with the adult noticing *their own* body signals: tight shoulders, quick breath, raised voice. Then using a simple regulating practice: slow breathing, grounding your feet, softening your tone. When we shift out of our stress response, our nervous system sends the message: "This moment is safe enough." That signal is the first step in helping a dysregulated student settle.

Offer Presence Before Correction

Instead of jumping straight to rules or consequences, focus first on curiosity. Get down on the student's level, keep your voice steady and low, and use brief, nonjudgmental language such as "I can see this is hard right now. I'm here to help. What do you need?" This step aligns with what Desautels calls *relational safety*—the idea that students can only engage their thinking brain when their body feels co-regulated by a caring adult nearby.

Co-regulate, Then Teach Skills

Only after a student's body and emotions begin to settle is it time to guide problem-solving or teach a strategy (like naming feelings, using a break space, or trying a breathing tool). Co-regulation is not a one-off technique; it's an ongoing practice of being a stable nervous-system presence around students. Over time, as students experience calm adults and then connection with the adults, they accept guidance from that adult to teach and their own self-regulation networks start to strengthen.

Key 3: Collective Commitments

If a classroom is a ship, expectations are its anchor. Without them, you're going to drift at the mercy of storms (conflict), strong winds (us shifting the tone in the room by not following expectations by mistake), and the occasional rogue wave (TikTok drama). Collective commitments are more than just "rules on a poster." They're a respectful agreement between you and your students that not only sets the course but keeps the crew on board, safe, and rowing in the same direction.

In our boat, we know how quickly a school day can go from smooth sailing to chaos. It takes only one group project meltdown or a misunderstood hallway glance to trigger a wave.

But here's the difference between a classroom that gets knocked off course and one that can right itself: shared ownership of clear expectations.

Rules are handed down. Commitments are built together. When students co-create the values and actions they want to see in their space, they have buy-in. And when they buy in, you don't have to micromanage behavior; the community manages it for you. Decades of research in educational psychology point to the power of **autonomy, competence, and relatedness** in self-regulation (Deci and Ryan, 2000). Students are more likely to regulate themselves when:

- They feel their voice matters (autonomy)
- They believe they can meet the expectations (competence)
- They are connected to others in the group (relatedness)

Collective commitments hit all three.

The Five-Part Commitment Cycle   The strongest classrooms I've seen follow a predictable rhythm to create, learn from, and revisit their commitments. The following steps can be used to establish a process if you don't have expectations currently and teach your students accountability and relational skills through the entire process.

1. Set the Stage: Build Psychological Safety   You can't expect students to share what matters to them if the room feels unpredictable or unsafe. That means starting with getting to know them, humor, and genuine listening.

Tell students directly: "Expectations are about how we treat each other, not about how I can catch you breaking rules." That shift in tone changes everything.

2. Name the Core Values   Invite students to brainstorm what kind of classroom they want. Record every suggestion without judgment; then group them into categories like Respect, Responsibility, Teamwork, Inclusion, and Safety.

3. How Values Translate to Behaviors   A value like "Respect" is abstract until you anchor it to behaviors:

- Respect = Waiting your turn to speak
- Responsibility = Coming prepared with materials
- Inclusion = Checking in on someone sitting alone

Be specific. Students can't meet expectations they can't picture.

4. Write the Collective Commitment Statement   Now you merge those actions into a unified, student-approved agreement:

"In our class, we listen fully, speak kindly, and help each other succeed. We own our mistakes and work to make things right."

Print it. Post it. Sign it. Treat it like the class constitution.

5. Revisit and Reflect   Commitments fade if they're not revisited. Build in quick check-ins:

- Monthly "Are we living this?" surveys.
- Reflection circles after big projects.
- Celebrations when the class nails it (like earning a group privilege or public shout-out).

Quick Tips: Clear Expectations Lower Stress

One of the most overlooked truths in behavior management is that clarity reduces anxiety. Many so-called "behavior problems" are actually "unclear expectation" problems. When students know exactly what's expected and have helped define it, they spend less mental energy guessing where the lines are.

Teach expectations the way you'd teach content.

- **Model it:** Act it out.
- **Practice it:** Have students role-play correct and incorrect versions.
- **Reinforce it:** Give feedback right away, both positive and corrective.
- **Visible:** Posted in the room, referenced in feedback.
- **Spoken:** Used in teacher and student language ("That shows responsibility").
- **Shared:** Parents and other staff know them, so the language is consistent.

What Could Go Wrong: When Adults Lose Their Grip on Regulation

We talk a lot about helping students regulate their emotions, but here's the truth: students are not the only ones in the room with a nervous system. Adults can lose their cool, and when they do, the impact ripples far beyond a single moment.

If we respond to student behavior inconsistently or emotionally, we send an unspoken message: regulation is optional. Worse, we model the very dysregulation we're trying to help students avoid. Imagine telling a student to "stay calm" while your own voice is loud with frustration. Students notice. They may not say anything, but their brains are keeping score.

Inconsistency undermines trust. One day a student gets a gentle reminder for a behavior, the next day they get sent out of the room for the same thing. For a student trying to learn self-control, that's like building a house on quicksand; they never know what's going to happen when they make a mistake. The unpredictability creates anxiety, which pushes them further from regulation.

Unregulated adult reactions can escalate situations. A raised voice, sarcasm, or visible irritation can flip a student's brain into fight, flight, or freeze. The moment we match a student's intensity instead of lowering it, we've handed them a model of conflict that relies on power struggles rather than problem-solving. Even if the student "complies" in the moment, the regulation lesson they've learned is that whoever yells loudest wins.

Mixed messages break down collective commitments. When one adult consistently upholds classroom agreements and another lets them slide, students learn that rules are negotiable depending on who's in the room. For a student practicing regulation, this is a recipe for confusion and frustration. They may start testing boundaries just to figure out where they actually are.

Students internalize adult dysregulation. The harm here isn't always immediate or explosive. Sometimes it's quiet: a student stops speaking up because they don't know how their teacher will react. A once-engaged student starts shutting down. A student who's been working hard to manage their frustration feels like their effort doesn't matter when the adults around them are allowed to lose control without repair.

If the adult doesn't resolve a situation where they caused harm, especially if identified by the student, it can fractal the trust in the relationship significantly. It can also teach them a maladaptive way for them to use in the future if they felt like they needed to. It's important for the adult to self-evaluate after a student expresses a concern, we see a change in behavior after one of our interactions, and repair any harm that might be there by asking "what do you need" through the perspective of curiosity in the relationship.

Say This, Not That

1. **Say:** *"I'm feeling frustrated right now, so I'm going to take a breath before we keep talking."*

   Not: *"You're making me mad. Just stop."*

   ☒ *Do* model naming your own emotion and a healthy coping strategy.

   ☒ *Don't* blame the student for your emotional state.

2. **Say:** *"We agreed as a class to speak respectfully, so I'm going to remind you of that expectation."*

   Not: *"Because I said so."*

   ☑ *Do* connect redirection to collective commitments.

   ☒ *Don't* rely solely on authority to enforce expectations.

3. **Say:** *"This is the same process we used last time, so we'll follow it now too."*

   Not: *"Well . . . I guess we'll handle it differently today."*

   ☑ *Do* be consistent so students can predict expectations.

(continued)

(*continued*)

  ☒ *Don't* change the rules on the fly unless absolutely necessary.

4. **Say:** "*Let's figure out what happened so we can make a plan together.*"

   Not: "*You're in trouble—end of story.*"

   ☑ *Do* invite collaboration to repair harm.

   ☒ *Don't* shut down dialogue.

5. **Say:** "*I hear you. Let's take a minute to cool off and then come back to this.*"

   Not: "*Get out of my room right now.*"

   ☑ *Do* use time and space strategically to de-escalate.

   ☒ *Don't* eject students without a plan for reintegration.

6. **Say:** "*I'm going to lower my voice so we can both think clearly.*"

   Not: "*Don't you raise your voice at me!*" (said while yelling)

   ☑ *Do* model the regulation you want to see.

   ☒ *Don't* mirror the student's escalation.

7. **Say:** "*This is a safe space for mistakes, and we'll work through it.*"

   Not: "*I can't deal with this right now.*"

   ☑ *Do* reinforce that challenges are part of learning.

   ☒ *Don't* emotionally withdraw from the moment.

8. **Say:** "*What's our agreement about group work? Let's revisit it.*"

   Not: "*You never listen when we do group work.*"

☑ *Do* focus on shared agreements.

☒ *Don't* make personal, global statements about a student's character.

9. **Say:** *"We'll keep practicing this skill until it feels natural."*

   Not: *"I've told you a hundred times already."*

   ☑ *Do* frame repetition as learning, not annoyance.

   ☒ *Don't* use past frustrations as a weapon.

10. **Say:** *"I didn't handle that as well as I could have earlier. I want to repair that."*

    Not: *(Ignore it and hope they forget.)*

    ☑ *Do* model repair and accountability when you make mistakes.

    ☒ *Don't* skip the chance to show students how adults own their actions.

Parent Huddle

As a father, I think the most learning moments I have with my son Asher is when I make mistakes and aren't regulated. He sometimes sees me in stressful situations at the end of the day when my battery is drained, and it's important for me to model that when I make mistakes, I own and fix them.

With him, I also often practice coping skills and learn how to understand when he is tired or has too much energy and how to strike a balance. We practice regulation as a family when we do things like these:

- **After a hype song is over, modeling how to calm ourselves back down,** sometimes through a preview and redirection of attention to the next task. Example: Turning down the music in the car about five minutes before getting home so Asher can regulate with less stimulation and pay attention when I share a task I'd like him to help with when we get home.

- **Playing a game together and handling winning or losing** in an emotionally expressive but safe way. If Asher yelled or tossed down the controller of the video game, I don't respond to this with an anger outburst but a direct redirection with understanding. "Do not slam that down again, if you break that, we will not be playing that again for a long time. I know that was a close game but it's just a game."

- **Exercising together and both of us taking complete electronic breaks.** We engage with each other with purpose and this is typically when Asher's most true questions emerge. It's where I see his greatest vulnerability, during our scheduled attentive breaks together.

In this parent huddle, I' challenge you and your family to come up with a list of tasks that you do that make you feel in sync and regulated together. Then make a list of activities or things that make you not feel in sync together. Discuss each list and how you can maximize the good activities and reduce the ones that create less connection. It's also important to create expectations around ways to deal with dysregulation or anger between you all as a family. My son knows that when we are upset at each other, what the boundaries are, and I model these with him and other people in my life and when I make a mistake, I model how I would want him to seek forgiveness also.

6

Modeling Respect

Navigating Defiance, Violence, and Unhinged Behavior

"If you don't underestimate me, I won't underestimate you."
            —Bob Dylan

Seek to Understand: Why Showing Respect Can Be Critical

I still remember the look on the custodian's face when she came up to me and whispered, "The kid walking toward us has a gun." My heart began to race as I looked over her shoulder to see a high schooler I didn't recognize walking down the hallway. Behind me was a group of students and staff having a pizza party.

She continued, "He was at the drinking fountain in the back hallway that I was cleaning, and when he bent over to take a drink, a gun fell out of the waistband of his shorts. He quickly picked it up and shoved it in his bag, not knowing I saw it."

Standing beside me were two colleagues: one teacher, Garrett, and one school counselor. I looked at them both and said, "I need you to trust me. The boy walking toward us might have a weapon on him, and I might need backup. I need to make sure he doesn't go into this room." They both nodded and walked with me toward the closest empty classroom.

As the boy approached in the hall, I said, "Hey, I'd like to talk to you for a minute. Let's talk here, where it's quieter?" He looked at me strangely as I put my hand on his shoulder and guided him gently into an empty room to my left. Garrett and the counselor followed.

As someone who grew up with guns, I knew how easy they are to use. I needed to stay regulated, calm, and close to him. Wanting to give the student an opportunity to share their side of the story, I kept my micro-expression blank and my tone as curious and even as possible and said, "I just gotta ask you something. I heard that you may have a gun on you . . . ?"

He pretended to be confused, but I could feel the tension increasing and his nervousness. Then he pulled it out, and tears began to roll down his cheeks. I felt every drop of nervousness leave my body, and I became hyper-focused on one thing: survival for me and the others.

The next few hours were a blur. The boy swung quickly from crying to yelling he's going to kill the custodian to laughing to pointing the gun at me. Watching his every move, I could tell that he wasn't stable as he paced the floor, rapidly changing his posture and tone. Like many educators, I was never trained in how to de-escalate a situation like this, but I knew my only real power was my voice and nonverbal cues. I had to speak with this boy with respect, from every angle of my words and actions, to keep things from getting worse. I kept mentally repeating these words: *I have to stay calm, I have to be assertive, and I can't let him hurt anyone.*

When he would say something direct like, "Was it that janitor who told you I had this on me?" I answered directly, "You know I can't tell you what I heard or saw on cameras, but I need you to hand that to me so we can all feel safe." To de-escalate, I did an empathy-connection to how others in the room were feeling, in case the student was dissociating, "I have these guys (motioning at the two educators) in here with me; they don't deserve to feel unsafe with you having that in your hand like that."

For the next few hours, I continued to maintain direct eye contact, watching his movements closely and breathing deeply out of my nose to keep my shoulders relaxed. I was very conscious to ensure that I was not frowning or giving away any micro-expression that could trigger the student more. I had learned from my father, who served in the Marine Corps, to recognize subtle cues of agitation, such as increased fidgeting and blinking. So, whenever I noticed things like how this student blinking becoming more rapid, I'd start to talk slower or say something lighthearted like "This sucks, bro, for all of us, let's just relax and I want to get some of that pizza in the other room before it gets cold, ya know?"

After this almost meticulous dance of language, keeping him from the door with slow gestures and bracing it with my foot, I was able to get close enough to grab the barrel of the gun while he held it down by his side. Looking him in his eyes, I said assertively, "Drop it. Now." He looked at me with tears in his eyes and let go. As I was taking the clip out and putting it in the teacher's desk drawer behind me, I turned around, and he had a hammer in his hand. There were several other weapons in his bag as the de-escalation continued, but no one was injured, other than a small stab on my leg when he threw his hunting knife down on a desk and it slid off and hit my shin.

So, what does this have to do with *you* and the everyday respect you need to see reflected in your classroom?

We aren't usually put into critical situations like this, and I hope no one reading this ever experiences what my colleagues and I felt that day. Nor am I offering this story as a how-to on de-escalating a potentially life-threatening situation. The reason I share this experience with you is that in this highly tense moment, I discovered the power and role that ***being calm***, ***acting* assertive,** and **modeling respect** can have in discipline. Sometimes we have to maintain our calm, assertive control with something as small as a student slamming their laptop closed a little too hard, breaking their pencil, calling us a "little bitch" under their breath, or whatever it might be.

Being able to regulate and speak to someone, while we are triggered, with a calm, assertive, respectful energy, not can possibly stop something bad from happening but can also help restore the peace.

The Challenge: We Are Confusing Obedience with Respect

My story is a rare one, and I want us to understand that the ability to navigate conflict is tough from the highest to the lowest stress situations. To better understand how to address unhinged and defiant behavior, I think the biggest question we must first seek to unravel is: Why do kids challenge authority?

First, we need to understand that obedience is *not* the same as respect. It is often mistaken for respect, but the two concepts are fundamentally different. Obedience simply involves compliance—students following rules or directions out of fear, obligation, or to avoid consequences. Respect, on the other hand, emerges from trust, mutual understanding, and genuine regard for another's well-being and perspective. While obedience may achieve short-term control, it isn't the ultimate goal. True respect fosters meaningful relationships, intrinsic motivation, and responsible decision-making.

Teachers asking "How do I get my students to obey?" might achieve temporary order, but asking "How do I build respect?" creates a lasting culture of empathy and positive behavior.

If our response is focused solely on blind obedience, we might not only damage the relationship and create a power struggle, but we also shut down a child's ability to think critically and feel safe standing up for themselves. Dominating a situation or coercing kids to command obedience is very different from earning respect. While respect looks different for everyone, it is rooted in valuing and acknowledging someone else's worth, even when we do not see eye-to-eye.

It's also important to show assertiveness without trying to flex dominance. *Dominance* seeks control over others, often through intimidation, punishment, or rigid authority, which inevitably leads to power struggles and resentment. *Assertiveness*, on the other hand, involves confidently communicating clear expectations, boundaries, and needs while remaining respectful and empathetic to others.

To find this healthy middle ground, educators must:

- **Express expectations clearly and respectfully**, framing requests as positive, collaborative invitations rather than commands.

- **Allow students to voice their perspectives**, ensuring they feel heard and valued, even when holding firm boundaries.

- **Model emotional self-control and consistency**, demonstrating that assertiveness is about fairness and mutual respect, rather than winning or losing.

When teachers embody assertiveness rather than dominance, they foster cooperation and mutual respect—preventing oppositional power struggles and creating classrooms that feel safe, fair, and supportive for all students.

We also run into a challenge when we try to force a student to respect us just due to our title or being an adult. We understand that some students may have learned a value like this and some may not have. If we focus on overcoming this challenge by teaching respect through our actions and modeling this for our students, they learn this more quickly. Mutual respect in a relationship is rooted in safety.

The Strategy: Model and Practice Respect

Respect isn't just about following rules or avoiding trouble, it's about understanding and considering the experiences, feelings, and boundaries of those around us. Just as violence can be a learned behavior and we teach empathy by being empathetic, kids also develop respect when it is modeled. To create a culture of respect, we must **define and practice** it with our students and help kids to **understand their triggers** by learning about the anger cycle. We also need to understand that de-escalation starts long before the behavior and requires us to **create authentic connections and relationships** before any situation.

Respect is understanding someone else deeply.

If we want students to learn how to respect others, we have to let them feel it. Kids don't learn respect through a quick YouTube video or a poster on the wall or even a rule we enforce; it's a pattern we model in our interactions.

Social learning theory reminds us that young people watch the adults around them far more closely than they listen to their lectures. Albert Bandura's work shows that we don't just learn skills by instruction; we absorb attitudes and behaviors by watching those in positions of influence we value. When teachers or school leaders show respect in their tone, their posture, and their responses to mistakes, students learn and start to copy what they see. When they see sarcasm, dismissiveness, or contempt, that also spreads just as fast.

The neuroscience that backs this. Our mirror neurons make us natural imitators. When students see adults listen without interrupting, acknowledge emotions, and set boundaries with kindness, their brains light up in ways that prepare them to do the same. When they sense disdain or harshness, their defenses come up, and they mirror that energy back.

Human reciprocity becomes a pattern. Respect builds trust and cooperation. Disrespect, on the other hand, sparks withdrawal, retaliation, or quiet resentment. These dynamics start to erode classroom culture.

Lastly, **developmental research tells us** that children who grow up experiencing respectful communication gain more than good manners. They develop a stronger sense of self-worth, better emotional intelligence, and healthier peer relationships. The same is true for educators: in a culture where they feel respected, they bring more patience and presence to their students.

So often I hear that respect means to be nice to each other, or we have a pre-conceived perspective of what respect has meant to you in the past like a "You need to make eye contact when I'm talking to you" type of mindset. But respect means something slightly different for everyone, shaped by their unique experiences and perspectives. To truly define and practice respect in our own communities, we can learn from this approach:

- Recognize that respect may look different to different people.
- Discuss openly and honestly about what respect means within our own community.
- Identify and practice empathy, understanding why certain actions or behaviors might make others feel respected or disrespected.
- Establish boundaries based on compassion rather than fear, focusing on mutual support and trust.

Respect needs to be taught with students who are regulated, have a mutual curiosity to understand one another, and have a common goal. We can create collective commitments as an entire class that define ways to interact with each other that don't cause harm, and if there is harm caused, we can agree on how to fix things in our environment.

Let's break down some of the best ways to model respect and de-escalate.

How-to Guide: Teaching Respect

Define What Respect Means in Your Classroom

These strategies can be between two people or between a classroom or staff circle.

Step 1: Making sure everyone is regulated, including ourselves It is easy to become triggered when talking about something like respect. You can refer to some of the practices in Chapter 5 if you notice kids or even yourself becoming agitated or dysregulated. Carve out time to have a safe discussion around this topic, creating an environment free of fear, embarrassment, or shame.

Step 2: Defining what respect means to the group and how to show it Allow each student to have the opportunity to share their definition of respect. Then have an active discussion and write a list of things you can do as a class to show each other you are being respectful, like making eye contact when someone is talking to us, speaking with a calm tone or facial expression, nodding our head when people are communicating with us, and reciprocating kindness when others are kind to us.

Examples to Practice During This Exercise:

- **Listening quietly without interrupting** when someone else is sharing their thoughts.

- **Acknowledging what others say** before sharing your own perspective (e.g., "I hear what you're saying . . . " or "Thanks for sharing that").
- **Asking clarifying questions respectfully**, rather than making assumptions (e.g., "Can you help me understand what you mean by that?").
- **Using respectful language and tone of voice**, even during disagreements.
- **Keeping body language open and welcoming** (e.g., facing toward the speaker, relaxed posture).
- **Allowing everyone a fair chance to speak**, even quieter members, by inviting them into the conversation (e.g., "We haven't heard from you yet; would you like to share?").
- **Respecting personal space and boundaries** (e.g., asking permission before giving a hug or high-five).
- **Offering genuine compliments or appreciation** to peers when they contribute positively.
- **Admitting mistakes and offering apologies** sincerely when needed.
- **Avoiding negative gestures or eye-rolling** when someone speaks to maintain trust.

Step 3: Defining what disrespect looks like to the group

We could then discuss what the group defines as disrespectful. For example, if someone doesn't make eye contact with me, that doesn't mean they don't like me or are being disrespectful. It might mean they don't realize that eye contact is a way to show they're listening. It's important to have this discussion with the group about what mannerisms mean to everyone, how to act, what to say, and how to navigate these situations as a group.

Students might collectively agree that disrespect means treating someone in a way that makes them feel less valued, unsafe, unheard, or uncomfortable. It's important that everyone clearly understands what behaviors fall into this category.

Examples of disrespect might include:

- **Interrupting or talking over others** when they are speaking.

- **Rolling eyes or showing dismissive body language** when someone is sharing.

- **Making fun of, mocking, or teasing** another person's ideas, appearance, or experiences.

- **Using hurtful language, insults, or name-calling.**

- **Refusing to listen or acknowledge someone else's feelings or perspectives.**

- **Violating personal boundaries,** such as touching someone without permission or intentionally invading their personal space.

- **Excluding or intentionally ignoring someone** in a group setting.

- **Laughing at or embarrassing someone** in front of peers.

- **Spreading rumors or gossiping** about someone.

- **Not respecting others' belongings or personal space,** such as taking things without permission or handling personal items carelessly.

Understanding the Anger Cycle

When I was a youth worker, I taught anger management courses every Tuesday and Thursday for a 10-week program with kids ages 8–21 who were labeled as "violent" or had violent offenses through probation or the courts. I did cohorts of my class for several years with groups of 5–10 kids.

I would always start the class by saying "Anger isn't bad. It's what you do with it that can be good, bad, or neutral." I'd also teach them that no coping skill will make you not angry anymore; it's just going to give you a second to think about what you should do before you act—and that pause plays a crucial role in our choices. Teaching these kids that the only thing they have control over is themselves was the best lesson we could give them. When you're getting arrested, it's not about what someone did or why you reacted; it comes down to you and your behavior.

The skills I taught these kids are something I still use every day, both when teaching and in raising my son. Making others feel respected is just that, a *feeling*, not just an action. We must remain regulated as educators and understand that if we don't model good anger management, we are not only causing harm but also teaching it.

The anger cycle is a model that shows us how our anger builds, escalates, peaks, and then comes down. The cycle offers an easy way for us to recognize our triggers and the cues, know when to use coping skills, and self-evaluate how we handled a situation when we were upset.

Step 1: Triggers   A trigger is a behavior, feeling, or thought that makes us upset. There are two types of triggers: internal (this is a thought, memory, physical sensation, or a feeling that comes from inside us) and external (this is an event, stimulus, or signal that comes from outside ourselves, something that someone else could see or notice).

- **Examples of internal triggers:** Feeling anxious, recalling past events, or having negative thoughts, feeling hungry, tired, or unwell

- **Examples of external triggers:** Being called a name we dislike, someone touching or hitting us, a facial expression that sparks a reaction, someone showing a form of "disrespect," or a loud noise

Take a moment to copy the following diagram to start to write out your triggers and follow along, with each step, to understand the flow of your own anger to be able to teach this to students easily.

The Anger Cycle

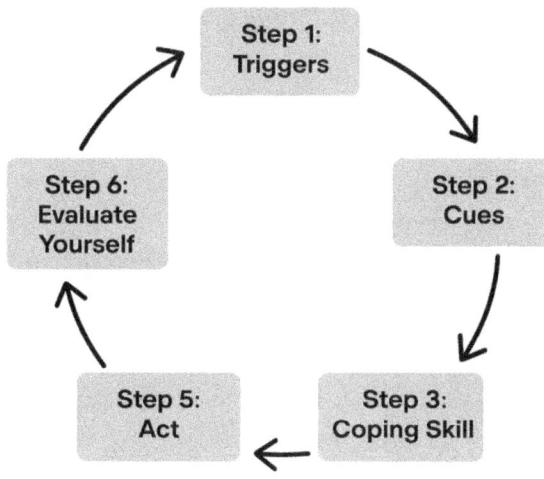

Step 2: Cues   A cue is a physical response or feeling our body has when being triggered or angry. There can also be internal ones (that happen inside you) or external ones (things you do that others can observe and see).

- **Examples of internal cues:** Our body feeling hot, our hands feeling sweaty, clenching our jaw, heart racing, eyesight narrowed into tunnel vision, ringing in our ears, and feeling tense

- **Examples of external cues:** Tone of our voice changes, body posture changes, we make an "angry face," clinching our fists, making a noise, or taking a visible and automatic action out of anger

In the same diagram, now list all your internal and external cues. This helps us understand that when our body responds in any of these ways, we are upset or becoming upset, and we need *to* do something about it. This can also give others insight that when they see these cues, it means you might need a moment as you continue to work through the anger cycle.

Step 3: Coping Skill   After we identify our triggers and cues, it's best to have a single go-to coping skill to use when we are upset. It should be something you can do anywhere, even when you're driving or teaching a class. Sure, it would be nice to sit in a comfy chair and listen to calming music with your eyes closed when we are triggered, but that probably wouldn't work out too well while driving or teaching.

You can jump back to Chapter 5 to reference specific tools that you can use to help facilitate a strategy to reduce anxiety and improve clarity into the perspective of what happened.

Write out your top three coping skills and try one for at least two weeks in a row before switching to the other one to find what works best for you. The goal of using the coping skill isn't to make yourself not angry anymore but to allow your brain time and space to think clearly for just one moment before you take action.

Step 4: Reminder   Choose a reminder or a vivid image that makes you pause. Picture an image or scenario that prompts you to pause before taking an action that could be harmful to yourself or others. Write this out in your diagram, and after you use your coping tool, quickly flash this reminder in your mind before acting. Choose either a positive or a negative reminder that strongly resonates with you.

- **Positive reminders:** Imagine the proud smile or comforting voice of someone you care deeply about, reminding yourself how your positive choices benefit those relationships.

- **Negative reminders:** Clearly visualize consequences, like hearing jail doors slamming shut, the cold metal click of handcuffs, or the disappointment on the face of someone you respect. Or imagining the pain you might cause a person or their loved ones if you do a certain negative harmful action.

Step 5: Act   This is when you can choose to act. It is the only part of this cycle that you have control over, so it's important to pause and self-evaluate: What action will you take and how might it affect others—positively, neutrally, or negatively? Then choose a regulated action that will not cause harm.

Step 6: Evaluate Yourself   Give yourself a score between 1 and 10 (with 10 as the best and 1 as the worst). Then challenge yourself with questions like "I am giving myself a score of 5, but what would a 2 have looked like?" and "What would an 8 or 10 have looked like?" This will help you recognize how things might have gone better or worse and think about ways you could improve in the future.

You can't control what triggers you. You can't control what your body does when you're upset, and you also can't truly control a consequence. The only thing you can control is how you behave/act.

I believe people start to disconnect from their own feelings and the feelings of others after not learning empathy, repairing harm, or having agency in the discipline process. What the anger cycle does is give us actionable things to recognize and the opportunity to make better decisions.

Scenario: Anger Cycle Use in the Classroom

Imagine you're teaching your seventh-grade class right after lunch. The room is a little restless. You notice Malik, a student who often struggles with impulse control, talking quickly under his breath while you're giving directions. As you continue talking, he suddenly blurts out, "This is stupid. I'm not doing it!" and pushes all his items off his desk.

At that moment, your anger is also triggered. Here's how the anger cycle helps you slow down and guide both yourself and Malik back toward respect and resolution.

Step 1: Triggers

- Your internal trigger is the thought "He challenged my authority and disrupted the attention in front of the class."
- The external trigger is Malik's defiant outburst and the sound of the notebook hitting the floor.

Recognizing these as triggers reminds you: "This is the start of the cycle. I can't control that this upsets me, but I can choose what I do next."

Step 2: Cues

- You notice your internal cues: your chest tightens, your face feels hot, and your voice wants to rise.
- You also see Malik's external cues: his jaw clenched, fists balled, and eyes narrowed.

By noticing cues in both yourself and the student, you catch the escalation early and ideally prevent either side from escalating it further. This is the moment to use a coping skill before either of you acts in a way that could harm the relationship.

Step 3: Coping Skill   You pause and take two slow breaths while silently counting to five. You keep your voice calm and even, even though part of you wants to react sharply. That brief pause gives your thinking brain time to come back online.

You also coach Malik, quietly saying, "Take a second. Let's talk about this in two minutes after I finish going through the instructions." You're not demanding compliance at that moment: you're modeling regulation and that you will seek understanding when it's an appropriate time.

Step 4: Reminder   You flash a positive reminder in your mind: "I want Malik to leave this classroom feeling like he still has dignity and a chance to fix this for me, him, and the classroom."

This helps you choose words that invite respect rather than fuel the conflict.

Step 5: Act   Now, feeling more regulate, you take action and decide to speak to Malik at your desk after you finished going through the instructions with the rest of the class: "Malik, I can see you're frustrated. Would you like to take another two minutes at the back table to take a break and then tell me what's going on or do you want to talk now?"

He says, "I just don't want to do this anymore; I'm sick of doing these packets."

You say, "I understand you don't want to do packets anymore but throwing things off your desk like that is hugely disruptive to me and everyone in this class. What could you have done instead, and how can we fix this with me or your class?"

Malik apologizes to you and admits that next time he is frustrated he will close his eyes and take a deep breath. If this doesn't help, then he will share with me his frustrations or where he is stuck separately after instructions for the entire class are given.

Step 6: Evaluate After class, you reflect:

- You give yourself a 7 out of 10—you paused, used your coping skill, and kept the situation from escalating, but you noticed your voice was still a bit sharper than you'd like after Malik shoved his things to the ground, but you still did excellent.
- You imagine what a 10 out of 10 would have looked like— slowing your breathing even sooner and using maybe a different opening line or potentially asking more questions while he was at your desk to understand him better.
- You plan to practice scenarios that could happen next time and responses you could use.

You also check in with Malik later and dive in deeper to teach the skill of self-evaluation, inviting him to reflect on his own anger: "What set you off? What did you notice in your body? Next time, what's one thing you can do before it gets to that point?"

Why This Matters

This is how we build respect in relationships: not by demanding it in the moment of conflict, but by *modeling* it, even in the face of disruption. Students watch how we handle our anger more than they listen to what we say about it. By using the anger cycle yourself and guiding students to recognize theirs, you're not just de-escalating one incident—you're teaching a life skill: that the power to choose our behavior, even in anger, is the foundation of respect.

Quick Tips

Here are my top five things to do to show you respect a student and to keep them calm when they are triggered:

- **Tone of voice:** Slow, steady, and flat.

- **Positioning:** Never block the exit of a room when speaking to an escalated student. Sit up or stand straight and show that you are present, actively listening, and engaged.

- **Empathizing:** You don't have to always agree, but they need to feel that you see their perspective or are interested in learning about it with your words.

- **Calm assertive communication:** This can look like using fewer words, lowering your tone, and keeping soft but direct eye contact with consistent breaks so they can look away and assess your body language.

- **Ask more questions than speaking:** It's always great to keep things simple or use open-ended questions to move conversation to more of an open dialogue.

Say This, Not That: Stop Saying "Calm Down"

⊘ Instead of Saying . . .	☑ Try Saying This . . .	♀ Why It Works	🌍 Real-World Example
"You're overreacting."	"This feels big. Want me to hang with you while we figure it out?"	Helps them feel seen, not judged.	A student spirals after a tough test—offer presence, not pressure.

(continued)

(*continued*)

⊘ Instead of Saying . . .	☑ Try Saying This . . .	💡 Why It Works	🧠 Real-World Example
"Relax."	"Let's try a breathing hack—smell the pizza, blow out the candle."	Gives a tool, not a command.	During a meltdown, shift into playful co-regulation.
"Stop crying."	"It's okay to cry. I'm right here if you need me."	Normalizes emotions & shows support.	A student tears up after a correction—don't shut it down. Sit in it with them.
"Don't be mad."	"Anger is a real feeling. Want to figure out what to do with it?"	Normalizes big feelings + invites problem-solving.	A student slams a book after a partner disagreement—help them channel it.
"Calm down!"	"You're safe. I've got you."	Regulates by grounding + presence.	During an escalation, keep your voice soft and your stance open.
"You're fine."	"This looks tough. Want to talk or just sit together for a bit?"	Validates the moment instead of brushing it off.	A kid's feelings get big after losing a game—acknowledge, then support.
"That's enough."	"Let's pause. What's your body telling you right now?"	Builds interoception + self-awareness.	When noise rises, help them shift back into self-check mode.
"There's nothing to be upset about."	"Something's bugging you—want to help me understand?"	Opens communication, closes shutdown.	When a kid is spiraling over group drama—go curious, not corrective.

What Could Go Wrong

You could walk into your classroom with every intention of setting a positive environment and five minutes later you find yourself snapping at a student because your coffee hasn't kicked in and someone just asked for the sixth time if this assignment is graded.

Here's the truth . . . even the most emotionally intelligent and amazing educators will make mistakes. *Often.* And that's okay. What matters is what comes next.

When the Teacher Isn't Their Best Self

Let's say you snapped, shamed, or just generally handled something in a way that escalated things. You can feel it in the air. The students shut down, or they are having an outburst. You lost the room. Now what?

Here's a simple (not always easy) model for repair:

1. **Acknowledge the moment.**

   "Hey y'all, I want to pause and own something really quick. I didn't handle that situation the way I should have."

2. **Take responsibility.**

   "I raised my voice. I didn't give space for questions. That's not the classroom I want to build with you."

3. **Explain,** *not excuse.*

   "I was frustrated, and I let that frustration spill out on all of you. That's on me—not you."

4. **Ask for help.**

   "I want to reset. Can we talk about what we all need right now to get back on track?"

5. Follow-through.

Maybe it's taking a two-minute breath break together. Maybe it's meeting with a student one-on-one after class. Maybe it's just moving forward, now that you've owned it.

By repairing out loud, you're modeling what accountability looks like with power and dignity intact. You're also showing students it's okay to mess up—as long as you make it right.

When the Student Isn't Their Best Self

Now let's flip it. A student has made the room tense. Maybe they lashed out. Maybe they shut down and refused to engage. Maybe they disrespected you or a peer. After the dust settles, don't rush to "fix it" with a punishment. Instead, invite repair.

Here's a quick student-centered script:

1. "What do you think happened there?"

   Open the door to the conversation, but let them tell the story in their own words.

2. "How do you think that affected other people in the room?"

   Build empathy without judgment.

3. "What needs to happen to make things right?"

   This is where they get creative. Maybe it's a conversation. Maybe it's a class apology. Maybe it's a behavior reset plan.

4. "How can I support you in making that happen?"

   Let them know they're not doing this alone.

5. "Let's check in after you've done that."

   Closure matters. Come full circle.

Repair doesn't require perfection—it just requires intention and repair. When we show students that relationships can be mended, classrooms can be reset, and one bad moment doesn't define us, we're not just managing behavior. We're building trust. And trust is the best classroom management strategy on the planet.

The Parent Huddle: Extending Respect Beyond the Classroom

Teaching respect in the home for me is when I teach my son manners and how to treat others through my actions and discussing situations together. We also make sure that when either of us make a mistake that we own the mistake and take action toward understanding how it impacted others around us. We also have to use a framework for understanding how to treat others with respect.

Understanding Framework to Teach Resect Start with curiosity and patience. When you hear about a problem at school, like your child talking back to a teacher or refusing to do work, pause before reacting. Gather as many details as possible and start by asking open-ended questions:

> *"What happened right before you said that?"*
> *"What were you feeling at that moment?"*

Avoid jumping to conclusions or rushing to what should be done. Parents also make a mistake by coming in defensive, either assuming the school is unfair or that their child is "misbehaving again." Instead of siding instantly with one version of events, show genuine interest in understanding the full story.

What *Not* to Do   Show anger too quickly, accept everything as fact without listening, or shut your child down with phrases like these:

"You need to behave or else . . ."
"I don't want to hear it."

These reactions can close off honest communication and keep kids from sharing what really led up to the incident.

The Shift   When you feel yourself getting triggered, even by your child's tone or by the teacher's report, this is your best time to model respect. Take a breath. Slow down. Practice active listening. Show your child that staying calm and hearing others out is a skill you value.

Instead of arguing or lecturing, say something like this:

"I can tell this upset you. I want to understand what was going on inside for you."

Your regulation is an active demonstration of the respect you're asking your child to bring into their classroom relationships.

Frame It as Skill-Building, Not Blame   Children often interpret correction as judgment. Shift the conversation away from blame and toward growth.

Instead of:

"You were disrespectful—stop doing that."

Try:

"I know you're still learning how to handle frustration. Let's practice some ways to pause before you speak next time."

You can share your own experience to normalize the learning process:

"I sometimes get frustrated at work, too. What helps me is taking a breath before I respond."

This approach tells your child that respect isn't about being perfect; it's a skill that gets stronger with practice.

The Plan   Work *with* your child to make a simple plan they can use at home and in the classroom. Co-creating a plan gives them agency and helps them feel safe coming to you in the future. For example:

- Step 1: If you feel yourself getting upset, take one deep breath and count to three.
- Step 2: Use a signal—like putting your pencil down—to remind yourself to pause.
- Step 3: If you need a moment, ask the teacher quietly for a break.

Revisit the plan together after a few days to celebrate progress and adjust what isn't working. Kids often feel powerless when adults argue over what happened or respond with anger. By showing curiosity, staying regulated, and inviting your child to co-create solutions, you send the message:

"You are capable of learning how to handle tough moments, and I'm here to support you."

This shared respect at home gives your child the emotional tools to practice respect at school and builds consistency between the two environments.

7

A Framework for Forgiveness

Breaking Through Labels, Repairing the Harm, and Creating Fresh Starts

"Resentment is like a chain that binds the soul. Forgiveness is the key that sets it free."

—St. Augustine of Hippo

Seek to Understand: Breaking Free of the "Bad Kid" Label

The first time I was suspended from school was in kindergarten, and I remember my best friend Brandon calling me "the bad kid" as a joke, but yet it seemed to stick with me throughout graduation. It was a label that stayed with me, even when my grades improved in high school and even after I made some major changes in my life.

I first learned how to fight at the kindergarten after-school program I attended at the YMCA "Beat the Streets." I learned maladaptive ways to deal with conflict early on and was not able to control my outbursts. Throughout my childhood, I remember doing things like breaking things often, self-harm actions, stealing, experimenting with substance use, fighting (verbal and physical), and lying. I didn't feel much fear around anything as a child. I had a significant amount of positive interventions and adults in my life that guided me over the years—but it still took time, and a lot of trial and error to learn, unfortunately for myself and for everyone I was negatively impacting.

As a kid who was struggling and who had experienced 9 out of 10 adverse childhood experiences, my sense of self was very delicate and confused. I had a lot of pull factors toward criminality, but I also had a pull for my high achievement. I could play five instruments, I was motivated to go to college, and I was doing well in sports. I balanced situations where I would take risks and harm people or myself and then had other situations where I could focus immensely to solve a problem. The thing that continued to draw me toward criminality was the lack of acceptance I received for being high-achieving. It was always shadowed by the label people had on me or the looks they would give me. I always felt "lesser" as a kid, and I needed to achieve to be noticed. I believe I mainly did criminal behavior to make myself feel powerful again, because I had no power in my other relationships in my life.

One person in my life that supported me well and held me accountable was my grandfather Bruce. He would sit me down while he rolled his cigarettes and talk to me for hours, in his rich Italian accent, sharing life lessons and how to be tough—and

I wouldn't want to even move a muscle. It was strange because at my house or school, I couldn't ever sit still. We had no technology other than a TV that we would watch VHS cassettes of *Jason and the Argonauts* and would watch reruns of old boxing matches as he would rewind and break the fight down for me. He was my best friend growing up and taught me how to play the accordion before I was five years old, and later the piano. Looking back at the reason why I listened to only Bruce, for a lot of my childhood, I understood intrinsic motivation is grown with people you have relationships with.

This label stayed with me throughout high school when I was accused of plagiarizing an essay for a scholarship. My teacher Mrs. Bennett had to prove that I didn't cheat by showing the judges my original draft that had significant grammar mistakes. I remember her coming up to me after and saying "Nathan, I'm so sorry they don't believe you wrote that story. I don't understand how you could have plagiarized; that was a story about your life and things you overcame." This was a scholarship that they gave to one high school senior girl and one senior boy, and I won the top spot in my high school. I went from almost dropping out and feeling like I did not belong to achieving my way to a fresh start and going to a university in a new city.

I remember it was my second year as a student at Purdue working toward my degree in behavioral neuroscience. I was aspiring to be a doctor at the time and leaned toward science with my first degree being analytical chemistry. It wasn't until I started working part-time at Cary Home for Children that I realized my calling was to help youth. I realized that I could quickly build relationships with the youth I worked with. I understood how it felt to achieve my way out of a label, to navigate complexities with family, and to constantly make bad decisions. After I graduated, I was promoted to be a full-time staff member on the violent offender unit. I worked there for my first seven years out of college, even as I overcame multiple health issues, including brain tumors on my pituitary gland and not knowing if they were cancerous. I kept working because I felt like it was my calling to not just share bits of my story when appropriate to mentor but to teach these kids better ways to navigate repairing harm and seeking forgiveness through actions.

The Challenge: Punitive Discipline Doesn't Offer Forgiveness

When labels stick with a person after they have taken action and have been forgiven by the stakeholders they impacted, it can start to cause a lot of additional harm. It can start to create feelings of helplessness. When someone is feeling helplessness, they also typically don't experience vulnerability well. This can even make it tough for them to communicate why they feel "off" or need support.

Think about a student or a child in your life and about how they would develop if they had no motivation to be successful, felt helplessness, and lacked the ability to feel vulnerability. This creates a lot of challenges for this critical development phase for children. If we believe that students deserve forgiveness and the ability to learn behavior skills like they have the opportunity to learn math skills, then we can develop restorative discipline tools to build behavior skills they might have deficits in.

Forgiveness in schools is often treated as a soft, permissive word. In philosophy, though, forgiveness is a judgment of identity and future possibility. It discusses that a person who failed is more than the failure and can pick a different next path. We live in webs of complex relationships, and she argued that forgiveness is the only way to "undo" the harm of past deeds, as we inevitably make mistakes in our web of relationships. When someone holds on to harm, it creates cycles as the harmed person dwells on the harm. It gets worse when we move to the spectrum of vengeance, which continues the cycle, but forgiveness gives us a new beginning. Without forgiveness, people become frozen in the past, stuck inside their worst moments.

As educators, without an opportunity for repair or forgiveness, resentments can build. But holding onto resentment quietly lowers expectations, narrows our ability to be empathetic, and teaches students that they are their mistakes. It also models the very dysregulation we're trying to help them replace. Without an opportunity to forgive, we may replay the harmful incident again and again in our minds, leading to rumination and putting us into a stress response, which can be exhausting. We may also become biased and see a student only as a label, rather than someone who is growing and still figuring out who they are.

Forgiveness is not the absence of consequences. In behavioral science, consequences are most effective when they are connected to the harm, when the student has the agency to repair, and when the adult signals a path to a continued relationship. That is what forgiveness looks like in practice and how students know that they still belong to a community even if they make mistakes. Inconsistent and random consequences can create pain and can push behavior change that leans on fear. Consequences that are linked to behavior teach empathy and skills. Like we discussed in Chapter 4, when an adult understands empathy as an accurate perception of another, consequences can be firm and humane at the same time. Punitive discipline asks, "What rule has been broken?" and "What punishment is due?" and not "Who was hurt?" and "How can we make this right?" It takes away a student's agency to make things right. Rather than accountability, shame is the driver, which can create denial, add to defensiveness, or shut down and block apology. It silences the person harmed, because it rarely opens the door to name the impact or what they need to feel whole. It can also fix someone's identity with labels like "problem kid," making a fresh start harder.

If discipline systems are built without understanding harm and seeking forgiveness, we will fall into the trap of relying on fear-based consequences to try to change behavior. It's important to make discipline simple for students and yourself. If you cause someone harm, you have to fix it with them. This chapter gives you a logical framework. Also, we want to understand why they did the specific behavior. This will then help them and us understand if there is a skill that needs to be developed or another resource needed to support making sure this harmful behavior doesn't continue. Through these processes we start to ask questions for the student to understand how to seek forgiveness by taking restorative action.

The other thing about punitive discipline is if an apology is required to be given, it often can become a performative, compliance-based script ("Say you're sorry!") that is driven by fear of punishment rather than empathetically understanding the others' experience. Often, once the punitive consequence is served and the "sorry" has been recited, traditional discipline considers the situation as "handled." But without reconciliation, meaningful and specific repair, there is nothing concrete to forgive, which can build tension between the relationship and cause those involved to feel dysregulated when they are around each other.

Neuroscience adds another necessary piece. When someone is stressed and dysregulated, the thinking and learning parts of the brain go offline—making it difficult to forgive and move on. It also makes it difficult to connect to empathy and repair. Bruce Perry's sequence that you learned about in Chapter 5, *Regulate* → *Relate* → *Reason* → *Restore*, is a simple and powerful way to help students return to a regulated state and turn this social system online. You cannot talk a thunderstorm into being calm. You help the body find safety (regulate), and then you build meaning through connection (relate), understand both sides through reasoning, and then restore. This is why trauma-informed, restorative approaches work better than punish-first: they create conditions for reflection, rebuilding relationships, and seeing the situation from another's perspective.

But, empathy can start to become overwhelming when not linked to compassion. Compassion moves us toward an *approach-oriented* state ("I want to help and set it right"), not a mentally overwhelming one. Adults who cultivate compassion are less likely to react punitively when hurt; they also can uphold boundaries with warmth rather than fear or anger. Compassion helps you to stay regulated and choose constructive solutions to move toward a fresh start.

Another challenge is that emotions can feel overwhelming. As Edith Stein insisted, emotions are not raw reflexes. They arise within and can be reshaped by the meaning we give to a situation and the processes we have learned for interacting with the situation. When we teach new ways of responding to conflict and triggers, we expand the available responses to feelings that typically feel overwhelming, so over time we start to respond more automatically with skill. We do not ignore emotions; we guide them toward helping us with clarity and understanding, repair, and growth steps.

The Strategy: A Framework for Forgiveness

I have long believed that forgiveness can be measured only as a feeling, not just a process. So many teachers around the world, across different cultures, have shared with me similar beliefs about how in theory it is easy to forgive, but in a situation after harm is caused, they don't know how to do this. So I have thought a lot about the framework to go through forgiveness to seek the feeling needed to heal.

My framework is simple and can be used as a self-guide or a guide to help instruct someone else.

Step 1: Framework

- **Name the harm:** Who (or what) harmed you, and how? Identify the specific moment, not just the person.

- **What was the context:** Where and when did this occur? Anchor the memory in its details: the season, the environment, your emotional state.

- **Witness the impact:** How did this impact others around you and in what ways?
- **Separate your entire identity from the harm:** Recognize that *you are not what happened to you.*

Step 2: Unpacking Emotions

- **Avoidance emotions:** In what ways have you numbed, denied, or distracted yourself from the pain?
- **Name the anger:** Allow yourself to feel the anger without shame; anger is evidence of your dignity and respect to self.
- **What is in the shadows:** What guilt, shame, or self-blame have you hidden beneath the hurt?
- **Trace the ripple:** How has this injury reshaped your health, habits, relationships around you and sense of self?
- **Shift perspective:** When you see the person that harmed you, do you compare your life to theirs? What does that reveal about what you still need in your healing journey?

Step 3: The Internal Alignment

- **Recognize your emotions:** Acknowledge that carrying this wound is doing to your sense of self and relationships.
- **Willing to start the process:** Forgiveness begins as willingness, not instant gratification, to a journey. Are you ready now for this journey?
- **Choose the path:** Declare, even to yourself, "I am choosing to forgive. Not to excuse, not to forget, but to free myself."

Step 4: The Restorative Work

- **Seek understanding:** Explore the humanity of the person that caused you harm. What pain, ignorance, or brokenness may have driven them?
- **Cultivate compassion:** Compassion is recognizing shared fragility in being human and making mistakes.
- **Embrace the pain:** Release the illusion that forgiveness erases suffering. Instead, carry the pain as transformed wisdom.
- **The future:** What do you want a future to look like with your life, and how will you release this harm in your life? Is it through a prayer, a kind thought, or a symbolic act. Sometimes giving loosens a grip of bitterness.

Reflection

- **Ask,** "What have I learned about myself, humanity, or love through this?"
- **Recognize** your own need to be forgiven. As you forgive, you join the human circle of mercy.
- **Know** that others have walked this road. Forgiveness links us to a lineage of survivors.
- **See** your story not as one of harm, but of transformation, to reclaim your purpose.

Forgiveness is not just about the offender; it is about reclaiming your own life, your joy, your future. Sometimes after harm happens, your sense of self becomes fractured, and safety is tough to rebuild. This is also an action of self-compassion to heal. If you aren't healed, it will be tough to support students through their healing journey, so self-forgiveness and understanding is important.

Research by Kristin Neff (2003, 2011) shows that *self-compassion* reduces shame and self-criticism while strengthening empathy. When people also forgive themselves, they're less stuck in cycles of guilt and more able to repair relationships with others. Self-forgiveness also improves our emotional regulation. Worthington and Scherer (2004) describe forgiveness (of self and others) as an *emotion-focused coping strategy* that reduces anger and stress. Regulated emotions make it easier to approach others with patience rather than seeking redemptive pain.

Once we know what it feels like to forgive, we can guide kids through the process of seeking to repair the harm and start anew. Here are four important reminders while teaching forgiveness that we must keep in mind:

1. **Regulate = feeling safe:** When the body feels unsafe, the mind protects rather than learns. Start every response by lowering threat cues and raising safety cues. Voice, posture, distance, and time that we respond all matter (Porges, 2022).

2. **The harmed person defines the repair:** Accountability is never abstract. It must focus on the impacted harm. There is never a need for performative shaming in a classroom, but rather processes and systems to unpack harm and steps toward making things right.

3. **Agency for students, even the one who committed harm:** If the adult facilitates all of the plan, the student learns compliance, not responsibility. If the student helps design and then executes the plan, the lesson was felt, and critical thinking skills were engaged to build empathy.

4. **Allow everyone to start fresh:** Forgiveness is real when there is a clear reintegration plan for the relationship. No one can do their best work while under a harmful label or feeling helpless within a relationship. Reintegration should include a visible fresh start that both can feel.

How to Guide: Five Strategies That Teach Tools Needed to Understand Forgiveness and Compassion

If we want students to understand what forgiveness feels like and to understand how to use compassion; we have to have the tools to build up to this in the classroom. The following strategies will help you get started or spark ideas for ways to integrate this type of teaching in your classroom or a small group setting in your school.

The Two-Minute Reset

Purpose   Restore physiological safety so thinking and empathy become easily available and to help regulate a group of students to bring clarity before discussing a situation.

How   Say in a steady voice, I think we need a quick reset. I'm going to breathe for four large breaths, and I'm inviting you to participate or sit quietly. Then you say four sets of "Deep breath in with your nose, hold it, push lots of air out of your mouth."

Why It Works   You are sending a bundle of safety cues. Using a regulated voice; a calm, nonthreatening tone; and paced breathing all help to regulate our physiological system and downshift any threat response. This is polyvagal self-care in action.

Link to Forgiveness   Forgiveness begins when a person can consider another perspective. That consideration is a heavy cognitive lift when the body is still braced for safety; the reset makes it possible to understand how to take space to regulate so you can take on maybe a more heavy cognitive load.

Let's Talk to a Chair

Purpose   Teach empathic perspectives without turning the harmed people into spectacles.

How   Place an empty chair between you and the students. Ask three questions in order. First, "What would the chair say happened in the room before the moment you were redirected?" Second, "What would the chair say the other person felt?" Third, "What would the chair say it needs to see to believe we are ready to start again?" You can also write the three answers in three short lines. Keep them visible during the repair plan.

Why It Works   Edith Stein's account emphasizes that empathy is perceiving the other as other, not as a clone of self. The chair becomes a simple artifact that holds that otherness and keeps the conversation out of a debate about who is right (Stein, 1989).

Link to Forgiveness   The chair lets the adult and student orient themselves to the harm and its needs, without the pressure of confronting another person in the situation. It is a clean path to understanding and action. This helps teach how to be curious with empathy.

"I Value This Relationship" Apology

Purpose   Start with apologies that focus on rebuilding relationship value rather than seeking performative remorse.

How   Coach the student to say the apology and add one thing they value in the relationship. "I am sorry for X. I value Y between us. Here is what I can do next." Adults can also model this same pattern when they cause harm.

Why It Works   Experimental work shows apologies promote forgiveness partly by increasing perceived relationship value. We seek forgiveness with relationships that we find value in, and this can signal to the other person that we value them, helping them move more toward vulnerability and understanding. The add one value line forces the speaker to name a shared stake, which changes how both parties appraise the future (Forster et al., 2021).

Link to Forgiveness   Forgiveness is built on actions toward repairing the relationships. Value language builds that relationship credibility and purpose.

The Fresh Start Architecture

Purpose   Make reintegration visible so labels and stigmas don't follow the student.

How   After the repair is finished, change one structural element in their day that signals a reset. Examples include giving them a new class leadership role, a new mentor check-in, or a reissued class job with a link to the incident. Announce only the new role, not the history of why it was assigned or changed to remove the stigma associated with harm or person that caused the harm.

Why It Works   Forgiveness is not just a private emotion. It is sometimes a public action. Arendt reminds us that action becomes real in a shared space. A visible role communicates that the person is back in good standing (Cain, 2023).

Link to Forgiveness   This fresh start is not just performative. It is a built-in system that moves us all closer to a relational focus, rather than just avoiding poor decisions.

Compassion Perspective Switch for Adults

Purpose   Reduce bias and fear caused by an adult's impulsive emotions in a moment or a situation that causes harm.

How   Before you judge why someone may have done something, silently name one specific potential alternative that could make this behavior understandable without excusing it. This sets us up for compassion and widens your response options.

Why It Works   Adults need actionable things they can do when hearing something difficult through an empathetic perspective. Creating an actionable practice with someone with compassion creates action and the ability for us to understand why to put ourselves in "someone else's shoes."

Link to Forgiveness   You have to fully understand a situation to be able to offer understanding and take action. So it's important for us to be able to stay regulated and seek facts while taking action.

Scenario: Using an Action List in a Middle School

The Harm   During a group science lab, one student, Marcus, gets frustrated and loudly slams his book on the table. In the process, he knocks over a water container, spilling it across the table and damaging some of his classmates' papers and folders. The lab activity is disrupted, and the group loses several minutes of class time. Two classmates are visibly upset, feeling both disrespected and set back in their work.

Teacher's Response Instead of giving Marcus detention or sending him out, the teacher calmly pauses the class, asks him to come to her desk, and says to just him, "Marcus, your actions disrupted your group and caused some harm to their work. We'll need to make an action list together so you can take visible steps to repair this and show your classmates you're ready for a fresh start."

The teacher then briefly explains the process, ensuring Marcus understands that this isn't punishment but rather about repairing the relationships.

Creating the Action List The teacher quickly jots down and hands Marcus a small index card labeled "Repair List" with three preprepared blank lines from a stack of premade index cards. Together, they quickly agree on three repair actions tied directly to the harm:

1. Prepare lab materials for his group so they don't lose more time tomorrow.
2. Tutor a peer on today's work during study hall next week to make up for the lost time.
3. Clean the lab station area after class today to restore the shared space.

The teacher writes them down on the card and explains: "Each time you complete one, I'll check it off. Once all three are done, the list is closed, and you've repaired the harm."

- The Repair Actions Same day: Marcus helps prepare the lab materials and then stays after class for five minutes, wipes down the table, and makes sure the lab is reset. The teacher checks off items #1 through #3.

- During study hall, Marcus tutors one of his peers who missed part of the lab because of the spill. The peer later tells the teacher, "That actually helped me understand it better." Item #2 is checked off.

The Power of Closing the Action List   At the end of the tasks, the teacher shows Marcus the completed card with three actions checked off. "Marcus, you completed your repair action list. The harm is repaired, and we're closing the list. That means we move forward from here with a clean slate. No one else has to get involved; you did an amazing job fixing this." The teacher then tears the card in half and drops it in the recycling bin, symbolically ending the process.

- Why It Works   The small, specific actions keep Marcus engaged in repairing rather than being weighed down by one large, vague consequence.
- His classmates can see tangible efforts of repair, which makes forgiveness easier because the harm is visibly addressed.
- The list itself acts as a neutral contract, reducing lingering resentment.
- Marcus experiences the felt shift of making amends and builds empathy by seeing his peers' reactions to his repair.

What Could Go Wrong: Protecting Against the Tough Side of Forgiveness

Forgiveness can be misused and abused. Adults can pressure harmed students to minimize pain or reenter too quickly. Students who are also desensitized can mimic remorse to escape consequences. Research warns that indiscriminate forgiveness, without actions, can enable repeated harm in relationships. It's important to teach that forgiveness is through understanding and acknowledgment, actions toward fixing the harm, and not continuing to do the same behavior. In school discipline, progressive consequences are the answer. Maintain clear thresholds and expectations where safety overrides reconciliation and insist that repair is action not only words.

Setting yourself up for success:

- **No forced meetings:** The harmed party decides when and if to participate directly.

- **Evidence of follow-through and actions:** An apology is never the end. It identifies the tasks needed with visible actions.

- **Progressive response for repeated harm:** Each recurrence adds additional structure and consequences.

- **School administrator thresholds** review when harm involves threats, weapons, bias-based aggression, sexualized acts, and severe injury, and follow safety procedures your school has in place closely.

Setting students up for success:

- Teaching a student how to set firm boundaries with others and why this is important.

- Teaching a student how to communicate feelings and what they feel uncomfortable around.

- Supporting peer-to-peer relationships with your students.

Try practicing a few of these boundary scripts with your students the next time they feel a peer has crossed a boundary. Join them in the conversation with the peer to help facilitate.

Boundary Scripts

Noise/Focus

- **Teacher:** "Boundary in one sentence."
- **Student A:** "Please keep your voice low near me. I need quiet to focus. If it's loud, I'll use headphones or move."
- **Student B:** "You need quiet. I'll watch my volume and work at the back table if I'm chatty."
- **Teacher:** "Agreed. Fresh start."

Teasing/Name-calling

- **Teacher:** "Name your boundary."
- **Student A:** "Please don't call me nicknames. I need respectful words. If it happens again, I'll involve an adult."
- **Student B:** "No nicknames—use your name. If I slip, you'll tell an adult. My plan is to stop the joke and apologize."
- **Teacher:** "Thank you—moving forward."

Taking Materials

- **Teacher:** "Set it for next time."
- **Student A:** "Please ask before using my supplies. I need my things during work time. If it happens again, I'll keep them in my pouch."
- **Student B:** "Ask first; you need your stuff. I'll borrow after you're done or get a loaner."
- **Teacher:** "Sounds good."

Group Work Roles

- **Teacher:** "Let's lock in roles with a boundary."
- **Student A:** "Please don't change my part without me. I need to finish my section first. If it happens, I'll pause the group and call you over."
- **Student B:** "Keep your section; we'll check in at 10 minutes. If I want a change, I'll ask first."
- **Teacher:** "Team plan set."

Phones/Devices

- **Teacher:** "One clear boundary."
- **Student A:** "Don't record me. I need privacy. If it happens again, I'll ask for the phone to be put away and tell an adult."
- **Student B:** "No recording. I'll keep my phone away during work."
- **Teacher:** "Done."

Time Boundary

- **Teacher:** "State your limit."
- **Student A:** "I can talk for two minutes, and then I need to work. If it runs long, I'll pause and finish later."
- **Student B:** "Two minutes, then work time. I'll set a timer."
- **Teacher:** "Great."

Online/Chat

- **Teacher:** "Boundary for messages?"
- **Student A:** "Please don't message me during class. I need to focus. If it keeps happening, I'll mute and tell an adult."

- **Student B:** "No class-time messages. I'll wait until lunch."
- **Teacher:** "Agreed."

To an Adult

- **Teacher:** "You can set a boundary with me too."
- **Student A:** "I'm overwhelmed. I need two minutes to reset, and then I'll start #1. If I'm still stuck, I'll ask for help."
- **Teacher:** "Thanks for telling me. Take two, and then we'll check step 1 together."

Quick Tips: Building Adult Capacity So the System Sustains

Even the best procedures fail without adults being embedded practitioners, as we talked about in Chapter 1. Here are quick tips for maintaining sustainability:

Five-Minute Staff Practice

Once a week, teams pair up and rehearse a two-minute regulation reset, a "talk to the chair" role-play script, and a fresh-start announcement. High repetition reduces hesitation to implement these strategies even under stress.

Compassion Self-Evaluation

At the end of difficult days, write two sentences. One names the challenge without blame. One names a student's effort you want to acknowledge. Short compassion reflection practices reduce empathic distress and help adults return ready to action even if mistakes occurred.

Parent Huddle: Allowing Fresh Starts

It is important for the home to be a safe place for students to explore their ideas and navigate the lived experiences they are having. If your child has a label attached to them from peers or adults, this is the space where you can help them navigate how to take action to remove this label or guidance with navigating it. Our kids will only open up to us about these types of things if they feel safe with us and understand that we will allow them to be in charge of their lived situations when they share these with us.

What Is the Ideal Environment for This Conversation?

I have noticed that my son likes to open up when we are both engaged and doing something physical together like playing a sport, exercising, or doing chores together. So I understand that sometimes when I have a big question on my mind that I want to ask him about, I know I need to create the space where he feels the most vulnerable so he will want to open up. It's also important for us as adults to have grace with ourselves and make sure we are also setting the stage for us also feel safe in an environment.

Showing Them You Are a Thought Partner in Conflict

When our children bring something to us, how do we position ourselves as their expert in their life for advice? It's important to support your children so they know how to speak up when they feel like their boundaries are being pushed or need help. If you look at your role as a parent as collaboration and support, how do you teach them skills to protect them? As a child, they need to understand how to communicate feelings and understand when to ask for help. If we teach this through safety, they will better understand how to navigate tough situations with a collaborator.

What Actions Are Needed for a Fresh Start?

Using frameworks, like my forgiveness framework, helps our children and us know how to navigate through conflict seeking a fresh start. It allows us to go through clear steps and a framework to try to spark the feeling needed for all sides to feel forgiveness and start fresh.

The more we allow our children to process situations with us as thought partners, the more we can help them understand how to learn these skills and navigate them. It's important to remember that the best learning is from our action and what we model in front of our children. So even in family settings like a car ride or dinner time, it's important to speak openly about family dynamics and how you are also navigating things without putting stress on our child but allowing them to learn from how you navigate even low-pressure situations that might require forgiveness or a fresh start.

8

Empowering Differentiated Thinking

Strategies to Support Neurodivergent and Disabled Students

"If you judge a fish by its ability to climb a tree, it will live its whole life believing it is stupid."

—**Albert Einstein**

Seek to Understand: Garrett's Story

Growing up with cerebral palsy, Garrett had a hard time finding his sense of belonging and uncovering how his differences could be a strength. Garrett and I first met him when I was a school administrator; he was one our best teachers and excelled so much that they promoted him to the admin team where we served together as assistant principals. Rather than writing his story for him, I've decided to share his words here:

Born three months early at 2 pounds and 10 ounces, my twin brother and I spent weeks at the hospital trying to get to our normal birth weight. In fact, I was so small that my leg could fit inside my dad's wedding ring. However, when I was young, I never perceived myself as "normal" because of my cerebral palsy disability. At a young age, I would find different ways to make friends and minimize my disability.

Therefore, anytime I was around individuals with disabilities, I attempted to distance myself. This desire to "fit in" started at an early age. I did not walk until I was four, so it was hard for me to play with my preschool friends. I would have to use my arms to drag my body around the room. If I could not go to the kids, I would make them come to me. I would collect all the toys around the classroom and hide them, so my classmates would be forced to come to me. Like many people with physical disabilities, I would find my own ways to accommodate.

In middle school, I continued to find ways to fit in. My disability required me to wear braces up to my knees. Not wanting to be seen as different, I would wear jeans every single day—even in the heat of the summer—to make my legs and braces invisible. I would not use any of my accommodations, allowing me to leave early for the next class, even if it meant being late. I would even avoid full-length mirrors, so I could not see the disability that others saw.

In high school, I would boost my self-worth in academics as I could compete and perform better than other kids who were physically normal. Competing in academics and theater groups, I was able to fill the self-esteem hole that kids with disabilities can experience when they compare themselves to normal kids. I think these self-esteem holes caused me to avoid dating in high school because of the feeling of rejection, thinking others viewed me as less attractive than my peers. These feelings around my self-worth existed for me until college. It wasn't until I was able to have honest conversations with other kids with disabilities that I started to understand that everyone has these feelings—regardless of their perceived disabilities.

—*Garrett Wilson; my friend, past co-worker, and extraordinary educator*

Garrett's story shows how the environment around us can either unlock or hold back potential. As a child, Garrett often felt out of place. His appearance made him stand out at an age when fitting in feels crucial. Early on, his perspective was narrow; he saw the world mostly through his own struggles.

That changed when he found purpose in education. Garrett's journey from a student navigating judgment to becoming a dynamic leader in high-need, complex schools shows what can happen when people find both passion and opportunity. Accessible environments and a belief in students' potential can open doors that might otherwise stay closed. Garrett later became a teacher on the south side of Chicago, where he developed a passion to support underserved populations. But what stood out most to me about Garrett is how he gave students a fresh perspective. He could relate to the judgment they sometimes feel because he had experienced it himself. That connection made his encouragement more genuine and powerful.

His story is a reminder that classrooms thrive when we adapt environments to students' needs, not the other way around. When schools focus on belonging and flexibility instead of enforcing conformity, students are more likely to discover their path and unlock their potential.

The Challenge: Classrooms Built for Conformity, Not Diverse Thinkers

Too many students are defined by a label or category rather than being understood for who they are. This is because classrooms are not always designed to assess students with different learning styles; we see clear need through the data for our neurodivergent students. For example, students with ADHD are more likely to repeat grades and face lower graduation rates. Dyslexic students are underrepresented in higher education, and having dyslexia can have long-term effects on employment. Autistic students face lower average educational outcomes, although many also display exceptional strengths in perception, memory, and creativity. Across different environments, studies consistently come to the same point: school systems still operate on narrow definitions of speed, standardization, and compliance.

Those who do not fit the mold are often seen as "behind," when in reality they simply have learning and processing styles that differ from others and should be seen as equally acceptable. This inaccessibility isn't typically due to a lack of trying from the educator but a lack of universal design strategies that support diverse learning.

It is also concerning the toll that misalignment, in a learning environment, takes on mental health. Masking, which is hiding traits to pass as "normal," is associated with depression, anxiety, and even suicidality. When teachers struggle with crowded classrooms that force conformity and require multiple interventions to track, some students are reduced to "problems to be managed" instead of being understood as humans.

If we measure children only by standardized performance, we risk missing their true capacities: the autistic student who can visualize systems others cannot see, the dyslexic student who excels in discovery and invention, the ADHD student whose entrepreneurial risk-taking sparks innovation. A deficit lens is not only harmful, but it is also inaccurate.

Today, one in seven public school students in the United States receives individualized support under Individuals with Disabilities Education Act. That is 7.5 million learners aged 3–21, which is roughly 15 percent of all student enrollment. These statistics tell us that neurodiversity and disability are not just a few cases; they are a significant population and part of the design problem every school must solve (National Center for Education Statistics [NCES], 2024).

Schools often don't recognize differences but push standardization and conformity. Those values start to punish students who process information differently, which feeds a deficit narrative that confuses nonconformity with inability. Inequity then compounds: national analyses show troubling racial disparities in discipline and access for disabled students of color, including higher suspension and law-enforcement referral rates (Losen et al., 2021). When race and disability intersect, behaviors are more likely to be misread or met with punishment rather than support causing harm to individuals' perspective of self, from a young age. This can also be part to blame on the accessibility of the classroom environment with differentiated learners and differentiated needs.

One way students cope to avoid exclusion is by masking or camouflaging. Autistic masking involves suppressing natural behaviors and adopting neurotypical behaviors to be accepted in classrooms and peer groups. It can be useful for people to navigate spaces they don't feel like they belong while being themselves, but this carries costs. Masking also contributes to late or missed diagnoses, especially for girls and women. Schools that mistake masking for "success" are rewarding a survival strategy that quietly drains the student from knowing who they are or feeling like being themselves even.

The Strategy: Empowering Differentiated Thinking and Seeing Students In Positive Framing

Asset-identifying is a simple strength-based way to define people by their assets and contributions rather than their deficits or differences. In special education, this shows up in strengths-based IEPs that start with what a student does well and then design supports to allow those strengths to carry more of the learning load. Strengths-based IEPs and person-centered planning are linked to greater self-determination, self-efficacy, and family engagement (California Health Care Foundation [CHCF], 2021).

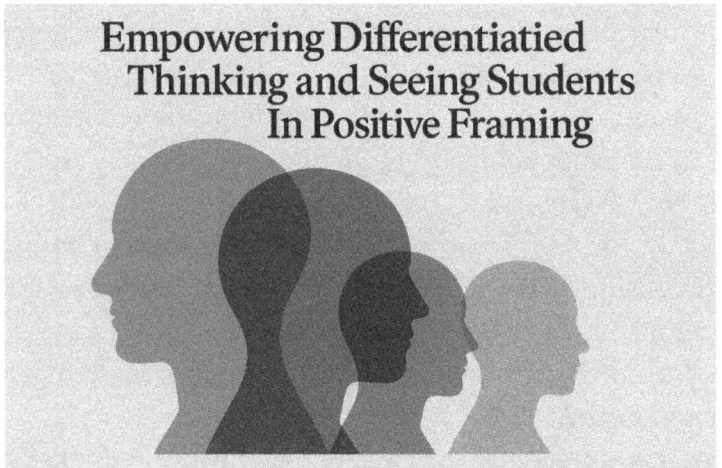

Positive framing is a cognition or thinking strategy that I love. Research shows that many dyslexic learners are biased toward explorative learning and thinking through a lens of innovation and iterations, which is something that schools rarely assess. Studies associate ADHD with entrepreneurial intention and action oriented, novelty seeking, and rapid ideation that can be channeled into productivity. Autism research shows a high prevalence of things like isolated skills and enhanced perceptual abilities. A classroom that never invites those assets into the center will keep mistaking potential for misbehavior. A classroom that uses positive framing will think about each one of these strengths as pathways to model or teach other students in that classroom. Can the autistic student model how to do mindfulness? Can the ADHD student help teach how to lead a group project? (University of Cambridge, 2022)

We understand to implement things successfully, the more we can use techniques that are universal and easy to do for all, the more easy we can keep up with them. Universal Design for Learning (UDL) helps educators plan for differences up front rather than retrofitting accommodations. The core idea is to have multiple means of engagement, strategies, and measurable actions. This is grounded in learning-brain networks. Use UDL as a design system and then evaluate impacts in different contexts in your classroom. Create ongoing checks that your choices are actually improving participation and performance for the students you target (CAST, 2024).

When I reflect on my own story, I remember being seen as the "troublemaker." Suspensions, referrals, and labels all reinforced that identity. What broke through to my motivation was not a program or a consequence but a teacher who sparked cognitive dissonance in my thinking through being strength-based. I also struggled a lot with my ADD in school with sitting still, paying attention, and being triggered with injustices. School didn't help teach me the executive function skills I needed but skills around compliance that I did not follow anytime it didn't feel "right" to me.

I was in eighth grade, sitting in after-school detention, when a math teacher who didn't know me well asked, "Nathan, do you want to stay here (in Marion, Indiana) for the rest of your life?" At first I had a gut reaction thinking that he was mocking me, but he was opening a door. For the first time, someone asked me to connect my actions to a possible future and showed me a path to something different. He didn't tell me I was broken or wrong or tell me what I should do. He let me think of two options: If I keep doing similar behaviors and show a lack of effort in class, what are my future options? And if I change my behaviors and put effort in class, what are those future options?

I asked him enough questions that I realized that I was able to have a fresh start as I started high school and that my GPA was my new best ability I had to control my own destiny.

Studies find that teacher belief and positive attention can amplify student self-belief and even self-accountability. Finding a pathway to passion in a college or career does not grow from accommodations alone but from relationships where students are seen for their whole selves and understand what they are good at and what they can do with what they are good at.

I think we will have a more peaceful society if kids, starting at a young age, understand their own actions and others through a perspective of empathy for others and self.

How to Guide: Creating a Strength-Based Classroom Where Masking Isn't Needed

Changing the environment reduces the pressure for masking, while changing our perspective of differences into drivers of learning also helps keep accountability intact. These strategies do both and are designed to be simple, repeatable, and respectful.

Create High-Support Environments

Predictable Visual Rhythms   Post a daily visual outline with images: start, mini-lesson, choice work, break, and exit ticket. This predictability lowers cognitive load for ADHD and autistic learners, and it prevents escalation due to being overwhelmed that would otherwise be blamed on "defiance." Pairing the schedule with consistent transition signals and words will also help avoid triggering students that crave predictability.

Sensory Environment Navigating Map your room for sound, light, and movement. Offer one low-stim zone, one medium-stim zone, and one high-stim option that does not add noise. Publish and practice the options so students see these as ordinary tools to utilize when feeling a certain way, not special accommodations for some. This lowers the need to mask and improves participation.

Positive Reframing and Helping Students to Identify Their Assets

Passion Mapping Sprints Every new unit of learning students begins with a 10-minute "map" where they annotate or describe the topic through their own personal interests. For autistic students, monotropism (the pull of deep interests) can be an amazing wellness resource and an engine to engage in learning. It invites students to see how their interests are intertwined with a concept, to help them gain a passion to learn about it in a unique way. This both honors the need to learn a similar unit but raises engagement for everyone.

Asset-Language Swaps Replace deficit language with precise, strength-based comments. Instead of "off task," try "likes stimulation and needs fast feedback loops." Instead of " stubborn," try "needs more processing time before switching tasks." Make these swaps explicit in IEPs, progress notes, and parent communication. Strengths-based IEP language increases student agency and family engagement.

Exploration Learning for Dyslexic Students   Every project includes a short "explore then explain" segment where students examine multiple ideas before narrowing into an answer. This aligns with research framing developmental dyslexia as a specialization in explorative search. This strategy can be universally deployed as a classroom circle discussion. So, not just the dyslexic students can explore before explaining.

Outlets for ADHD   Offer competitive micro-challenges in class through things like a classroom reward system, a competition with a project, or even leadership and teaching opportunities to help teach the class. Brief challenges like this capture novelty seeking and reward rapid ideas, channeling traits associated with entrepreneurial action and ADHD reward centers for the brain.

Provide Developmentally Brain-Aligned Discipline

Accountability and consistency are essential for success while using discipline. The question is how to deliver it so students actually learn from it and do not need to become anxious or fear driven. Holding students accountable is still essential. But accountability for neurodivergent and disabled students must be shaped by how their brains process information and stress. A one-size-fits-all punishment approach not only fails—it often escalates behaviors.

- **Autistic students** may struggle with transitions and sensory overload. Discipline should focus on predictability, clarity, and de-escalation, not confrontation. Offer structured routines and use visual social narratives to preview expectations, and then connect any consequence to restoring safety or time lost, not to humiliation or causing shame.

Masking often intensifies after public reprimands; keep repair private and concrete.

- **ADHD students** may act impulsively, not maliciously. Discipline works best when linked to immediate, logical consequences that redirect energy productively rather than delayed punishments. Delay and distance reduce learning; redirect energy into a helpful role within the same period when possible.

- **Dyslexic students** may experience shame in literacy-heavy tasks. Accountability should not be about exposing weaknesses publicly but ensuring supports like audio, dictation, or alternative demonstrations of mastery.

- **Students with emotional or behavioral disabilities** may require black-and-white choices, especially where emotional dysregulation overwhelms executive function. Research in dialectical behavioral therapy shows that clarity, not complexity, is key.

The goal is not to excuse harm but to differentiate accountability. Logical consequences must align with how the student's brain works so they can learn from the moment instead of being trapped by it.

Build a Classroom That Makes Masking Unnecessary

Student safety perspectives grow from watching us through thousands of small cues we don't even know we are exhibiting sometimes. It's important to focus and do things like make eye contact with people in wheelchairs naturally as you would with anyone else. Normalize assistive accommodations and tech by using it yourself and not making comments about it jokingly or just overall. Rotate how students participate so things like talking is not the only accepted currency of participation. Inclusion is

not just a word or one strategy in a classroom. It is active empowerment and the way we assess learning.

The previous strategies are highlighted in these four pillars
of research:

1. **Strengths-based approaches** stop defining students by deficits and establish a positive sense of identity. When we build
   assignments that let students leverage their unique strengths,
   they move from conformity to diverse contributions.

2. **Student-driven processes:** Invite students into decisions
   about how they learn best and assess what's working to
   increase ownership.

3. **Skills and resilience building:** Teach coping strategies, not
   just academic strategies to learn. Executive function coaching, emotional regulation tools, and restorative practices all
   expand capacity for inclusivity.

4. **Connection and belonging:** Circles, peer partnerships, and
   teacher–student strategies of recognition make students feel
   part of a community that wants them there.

The Unmasking Feedback Loop   Teach students the language to name and understand masking. Once a week, run a two-
minute private check-in. Let students pick the format to share
this; maybe it's a quick talk, sticky note, or 30-second audio
note. Ask them:

- When did you feel you had to hide how your brain works or
  who you are?

- What is one change we can make so you do not have to do
  that as much?

This could turn into a discussion that can help you design or
architect your classroom environment differently. The goal is

not to stop masking but to reduce the environmental demand for it. Research links camouflaging to mental-health costs; reducing the need to mask is a protective mental-health strategy.

Quick Tips for Proactive Engagement

Pair students thoughtfully. Sometimes similar learners provide safety; other times, mixed abilities encourage growth. It's also important to avoid overburdening high-performing peers with constant "buddy" responsibilities.

What Could Go Wrong

If teachers only adjust the environment but do not build systems to sustain these practices, things could start to become inconsistent. The students may even start to become more dysregulated with the lack of consistency and predictability.

If discipline focuses on conformity and fear, it goes against brain development, and consequences become traumatizing rather than corrective lessons. And if inclusion turns into tokenism strategies, it sets up disabled students to feel even more ostracized, which can become worse if they also feel internally different too.

UDL can become a checklist rather than a design process; evaluate whether your multiple options actually improved access for the students you are focused on supporting. Asset-framing must not erase real barriers or a skill that still needs to be developed. If a student seems fine in your class and falls apart elsewhere, investigate: there may be a skill that needs to be developed with them or an environment that needs to understand them differently.

Parent Huddle

In the home we understand that interactions with family plays a critical role in reinforcing the development of self for your child. Kids are constantly challenging authority, pushing boundaries, learning through failure, and having fun. We have to find the balance of letting a kid be themselves, different or part of a group, and understand that their childhood is a discovery journey of them understanding themselves and that we as adults are their guides.

When we start to celebrate the journey over the outcome, your child also starts to understand and celebrate the journey more than the outcomes. They start to identify things that fill their cup and things that make them feel like they have to mask or conform. This is such a critically important part of childhood and development of personality. A lot of long-term success for even adults is determined by how quickly they can understand themselves and their passions.

Here are some strategies to bring these practices into the home and help with self-exploratory processes:

- **Use family circles:** Give each member a turn to share and determine a discussion topic. This builds communication skills, ability to lead discussions, healthy ways to explore topics with family, and teaching empathy by listening to others in the circle.

- **Normalize differences:** Talk openly about situations you come across so children do not internalize differences as shameful.

- **Model accessible problem-solving:** When something is hard, show how you adapt and how there are multiple paths of differentiated thinking to get to a solution. You can do this using a checklist, asking for different perspective mapping, or breaking tasks into steps before focusing on the solution.

- **Collaborate with educators in the school:** Share what works at home and listen to what works in the school. Consistency across settings reduces stress and helps with quicker development of skills for success.

It's important to establish the home as a learning ground and an exploratory safe time to process things without judgment. Family establishes culture, values, and development of a sense of self. As parents, when we establish clear processes that are consistent, we can navigate conflict or uncertainty more easily. We become proactive and preventative with situations by teaching our children these skills.

When we look at our children as special, not by how they act but by who they are (how they learn, how they think, how they have fun), we help them understand and develop their own perspectives of self. This helps with them accepting themselves even if they might be looked at physically or cognitively differently, which I believe will help them accept others more easily also.

I remember as a kid that I saw a man walking with a limp and said to my dad, "That guy walks weird." My dad laughed and looked at me and said, "What's weird? I bet he thinks you walk weird."

Conclusion: Empathy Is Our Connection Thread

The memory of being misunderstood, mislabeled, and underestimated has driven me to seek to understand the kids I've worked with. As I said in the introduction, my goal for this book is to help you navigate the frustrating, complex, and unhinged behaviors we see in schools. I hope you take some of these stories from the work I've done and lessons I've learned in my life as motivation to take action even in small interactions you have with others.

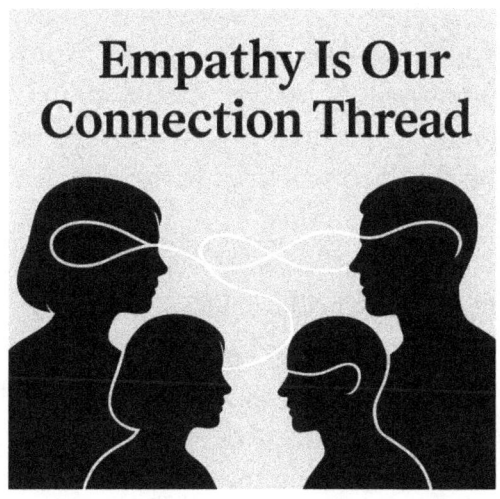

Empathy Is Our Connection Thread

The belief that discipline has to be painful to change behaviors isn't just wrong; it's harmful. I've seen this through working directly in hundreds of some of the most challenging schools in the United States since my first book, *Hacking School Discipline*, was released. I also see this in data trends as I have advised large-impact organizations and government entities around the world supporting schools. It's important for us to understand that this work isn't about large shifts; it's about small ones. These small shifts start in our interactions with people around us, and understanding this is the best teaching. We are using discipline as a tool for motivation and true change in negative patterns of behaviors. When we use fear to change behavior, we create negative experiences during a learning moment for kids as they are trying to develop who they are.

Throughout the book we intertwined tools that teach empathy, forgiveness, and belonging into an equation. We also know that these aren't things that can stand alone without us doing something with these feelings and seeing around the "corners." Empathy needs compassion to be actionable or it weighs on us. Forgiveness needs actions with logical consequences and accountability within the relationship. Belonging can be positive or negative with either pulling toward criminal behavior or conformity without deep connection with self-identified purpose already established.

As a past school administrator, I understand the importance of positively impacting the individual (educator or student or parent) and also impacting the system (school culture, policies, plans, and community school is in). We can't just zoom in or zoom out as school administrators—we have responsibilities for both individuals and the system. My co-founder of Highfive, Dr. Luke Roberts, earned his PhD in systems complexity theory at Cambridge University, and I've learned an immense amount of knowledge from him about how to change systems. I've learned that we should start with intentionality with what behaviors we do that impact the system, evaluation of how things impact the system and what success metrics we need to look for, and how we can look at the environment as a living breathing ecosystem.

I strongly feel that teaching students empathy perspectives and actionable compassion will help lower violence not just in schools but society. We need more people that care about each other and understand how behaviors impact each other on a deep level. If we start small, by teaching through modeling with the way we treat others, we can change the world with one interaction at a time by building empathy in our kids.

The Navajo Nation's *seven generations* teaching says that every choice we make should honor those who came before us and protect those who come after. This comes out to roughly 175 years of impact in every large decision we make. When I learned this, before Highfive partnered with one of their school districts in New Mexico, from my friend and fellow expert that I worked with for several years, Dr. Ben Lester, it reframed a lot for me. Teaching empathy isn't just about one school year' it's about changing the human story. Every time a student chooses understanding over harm, we're shaping the next seven generations to inherit a world built on curiosity for understanding, not fear.

Bibliography

American Psychological Association Task Force. (2008). Are zero tolerance policies effective in the schools? An evidentiary review and recommendations. *American Psychological Association*. https://www.apa.org/pubs/info/reports/zero-tolerance.

Ampofo, J., Bentum-Micah, G., Xusheng, Q., Sun, B., & Mensah Asumang, R. (2025). Exploring the role of teacher empathy in student mental health outcomes: A comparative SEM approach to understanding the complexities of emotional support in educational settings. *Frontiers in Psychology*, *16*, 1503258. https://doi.org/10.3389/fpsyg.2025.1503258.

Breese, A. C., Nickerson, A. B., Lemke, M. et al. (2023). Examining implicit biases of pre-service educators within a professional development context. *Contemp School Psychol*, *27*, 646–661. https://doi.org/10.1007/s40688-023-00456-6.

Cain, A. (2023). 'The Wheel is Crooked': Hannah Arendt on action, success and public happiness. *HannahArendt.Net*, *13*(1), 82–96. https://www.hannaharendt.net/index.php/han/article/view/535/891.

California Health Care Foundation. (2021, April). *Understanding asset-framing: Guidelines for CHCF authors*. https://www.chcf.org/wp-content/uploads/2021/04/UnderstandingAssetFramingGuidelinesAuthors.pdf.

CAST. (2024). *Universal Design for Learning Guidelines, version 3.0*. Retrieved from https://udlguidelines.cast.org/.

Deci, E. L., & Ryan, R. M. (2000). Self-determination theory and the facilitation of intrinsic motivation, social development, and well-being. *American Psychologist*, *55*(1), 68–78. https://doi.org/10.1037/0003-066X.55.1.68.

Eisenberg, N., Spinrad, T. L., & Eggum, N. D. (2010). Emotion-related self-regulation and its relation to children's maladjustment. *Annual Review of Clinical Psychology*, *6*, 495–525. https://doi.org/10.1146/annurev.clinpsy.121208.131208.

Forster, D. E., Graham, J. E., Churches, E., Karremans, J. C., & Van Lange, P. A. M. (2021). Experimental evidence that apologies promote forgiveness by communicating relationship value. *Frontiers in Psychology, 12,* 724789. https://doi.org/10.3389/fpsyg.2021.724789.

Fredrickson, B. L., Grewen, K. M., Algoe, S. B., Firestine, A. M., Arevalo, J. M. G., Ma, J., & Cole, S. W. (2015). Psychological well-being and the human conserved transcriptional response to adversity. *PLoS ONE 10*(3): e0121839. https://doi.org/10.1371/journal.pone.0121839.

Gunnar, M. R., & Quevedo, K. (2007). The neurobiology of stress and development. *Annual Review of Psychology, 58,* 145–173. https://doi.org/10.1146/annurev.psych.58.110405.085605.

Hough, L. (2022, September 30). *Why psychological safety matters in class.* Harvard Graduate School of Education. https://www.gse.harvard.edu/ideas/news/22/09/why-psychological-safety-matters-class.

Jennings, P. A., & Greenberg, M. T. (2009). The prosocial classroom: Teacher social and emotional competence in relation to student and classroom outcomes. *Review of Educational Research, 79*(1). https://doi.org/10.3102/0034654308325693.

Losen, D. J., Martinez, P., & Shin, G. H. R. (2021, March 22). *Disabling inequity: The urgent need for race-conscious resource remedies.* The Center for Civil Rights Remedies at the Civil Rights Project, UCLA. Retrieved November 11, 2025, from https://civilrightsproject.ucla.edu/wp-content/uploads/2021/03/final-Report-03-22-21-v5-corrected.pdf.

Masten, A. S. (2014). *Ordinary Magic: Resilience in Development.* The Guilford Press.

McCrory, E., De Brito, S. A., & Viding, E. (2011). The impact of childhood maltreatment: A review of neurobiological and genetic factors. *Frontiers in Psychiatry, 2,* 48. https://doi.org/10.3389/fpsyt.2011.00048.

National Center for Education Statistics. (2024). *Students with disabilities* (Indicator: "CGG"). In *Condition of Education.* U.S. Department of Education, Institute of Education Sciences. Retrieved November 11, 2025, from https://nces.ed.gov/programs/coe/indicator/cgg/students-with-disabilities.

Neff, K. D. (2003). Self-compassion: An alternative conceptualization of a healthy attitude toward oneself. *Self and Identity, 2*(2), 85–101. https://doi.org/10.1080/15298860309032.

Neff, K. D. (2011). *Self-Compassion: The Proven Power of Being Kind to Yourself.* William Morrow.

Okonofua, J. A., Goyer, J. P., Lindsay, C. A., Haugabrook, J., & Walton, G. M. (2022). A scalable empathic-mindset intervention reduces group disparities in school suspensions. *Science Advances, 8*(12), eabj0691. https://doi.org/10.1126/sciadv.abj0691.

Pianta, R. C., Hamre, B. K., & Allen, J. P. (2012). *Teacher-student relationships and engagement: Conceptualizing, measuring, and improving the capacity of classroom interactions.* In S. L. Christenson, A. L. Reschly, & C. Wylie (Eds.), *Handbook of Research on Student Engagement* (pp. 365–386). Springer. https://doi.org/10.1007/978-1-4614-2018-7_17.

Porges, S. W. (2022, May 10). Polyvagal Theory: A science of safety. *Frontiers in Integrative Neuroscience, 16,* 871227. https://doi.org/10.3389/fnint.2022 .871227.

Roeser, R. W., Schonert-Reichl, K. A., Jha, A., Cullen, M., Wallace, L., Wilensky, R., Oberle, E., Thomson, K., Taylor, C., & Harrison, J. (2013). Mindfulness training and reductions in teacher stress and burnout: Results from two randomized, waitlist-control field trials. *Journal of Educational Psychology, 105*(3), 787–804. https://doi.org/10.1037/a0032093.

Smith, L. J., Thompson, R. J., & Hartley, C. A. (2023). Daily emotion regulation and mood instability in adults with histories of childhood maltreatment. *Nature Human Behaviour.* https://doi.org/10.1038/s41562-023-01532-1.

Stein, E. (1989). *On the problem of empathy* (W. Stein, Trans.; 3rd rev. ed.). ICS Publications. (Original work published 1917)

Teicher, M. H., & Samson, J. A. (2016). Annual research review: Enduring neurobiological effects of childhood abuse and neglect. *Journal of Child Psychology and Psychiatry, 57*(3), 241–266. https://doi.org/10.1111/jcpp .12507.

University of Cambridge. (2022, June 24). *Developmental dyslexia essential to human adaptive success, study argues.* Retrieved November 11, 2025, from https://www.cam.ac.uk/research/news/developmental-dyslexia-essential-to-human-adaptive-success-study-argues.

University of Essex. (2024). *Childhood Trauma Linked to Rewired Brain Circuits in Largest Neuroimaging Study to Date.* University of Essex Research Bulletin.

World Health Organization. (2023). WHO Commission on Social Connection: Addressing loneliness as a pressing health threat. *World Health Organization.* https://www.who.int/groups/commission-on-social-connection.

Worthington, E. L., & Scherer, M. (2004). Forgiveness is an emotion-focused coping strategy that can reduce health risks and promote health resilience: Theory, review, and hypotheses. *Psychology & Health, 19*(3), 385–405. https://doi.org/10.1080/0887044042000196674.

Zoogman, S., Goldberg, S. B., Hoyt, W. T., & Miller, L. (2015). Mindfulness interventions with youth: A meta-analysis. *Mindfulness, 6*(2), 290–302. https://doi.org/10.1007/s12671-013-0260-4.

Additional Resources

Scan to receive free tools from *Science of Discipline*—a gift from Nathan Maynard to help educators build calmer, more connected, and resilient classroom communities.

Acknowledgments

First, I want to acknowledge my biggest mentor, Jesus Christ. Your teachings of forgiveness, empathy, and belonging will always be my guiding principles of how I walk my life on this planet and show your work through my interactions and not just words.

Second, to my son, Asher: you have been my reminder that healing is generational work. You show me what the next seven generations deserve. Thank you for being the light that guides every page of this book. I can't wait to read your book one day. Thank you for all the time you have shared me with educators all over the world. I've healed a lot of people with you as my north star.

To the educators who walked this journey with me. The ones who tried new practices, stayed patient, and believed that relationships could transform classroom dynamics, thank you for taking care of our children.

To the school leaders and district teams who opened their doors, gave me space to coach, and helped Highfive take roots to globally add tools to the discipline toolkits of educators. Your courage shaped this book.

To my Highfive team, past and present, from Restorative Group Consulting across the world to BehaviorFlip to the

250,000 educators who read my book to the data thinkers, curriculum builders, software engineers, program directors, and partners who built this movement brick by brick. Your brilliance and belief continue to expand what we thought was possible in schools.

To the thinkers who shaped my understanding of trauma, belonging, and the human mind like Lori Deaustels, Bruce Perry, Dan Siegel, Edith Stein, the Navajo educators who taught me the seven generations principle, and my elders and mentors who continue to expand my understanding of healing and responsibility.

This book was built from thousands of moments with young people who trusted me enough to let me into their stories. To every youth that taught me what empathy really feels like through the most complexities of life. You are the heartbeat and my motivation for all my work.

And finally, to everyone who believes in, supports, uplifts, and loves the children we have the opportunity to impact their lives.

Index